MW00466731

Classification in the Wild

Classification in the Wild

The Science and Art of Transparent Decision Making

Konstantinos V. Katsikopoulos, Özgür Şimşek, Marcus Buckmann, and Gerd Gigerenzer

The MIT Press
Cambridge, Massachusetts
London, England

This book was set in Stone Serif and Stone Sans by Jen Jackowitz. Printed and bound in the United States of America.

Library of Congress Cataloging-in-Publication Data

Names: Katsikopoulos, Konstantinos V., author.
Title: Classification in the wild : the science and art of transparent
    decision making / Konstantinos V. Katsikopoulos, Özgür
    Şimşek, Marcus Buckmann, and Gerd Gigerenzer.
Description: Cambridge, Massachusetts : The MIT Press, [2020] | Includes
    bibliographical references and index.
Identifiers: LCCN 2020015193 | ISBN 9780262045155 (hardcover)
Subjects: LCSH: Categorization (Psychology)—Case studies. |
    Classification—Case studies. | Uncertainty—Case studies.
Classification: LCC BF445 .K38 2020 | DDC 001.01/2—dc23
LC record available at https://lccn.loc.gov/2020015193

10 9 8 7 6 5 4 3 2 1

To our families

Contents

Acknowledgments

This book benefited greatly from the input provided by many colleagues. We are grateful to David Aikman, Jerome Busemeyer, Jean Czerlinski Whitmore, Uwe Czienskowski, Dan Goldstein, Panagiotis Katsikopoulos, Niklas Keller, Jan Malte Lichtenberg, Shenghua Luan, Laura Martignon, Douglas Medin, Nancy Montgomery, Christophe Mues, Nathaniel Phillips, Lael Schooler, Leonidas Spiliopoulos, and Leighton Vaughan Williams. We are indebted to Gisela Henkes for administrative help and Rona Unrau for suggestions on the writing. Finally, we would like to extend a big thanks to Philip Laughlin, Judy Feldmann, and Alex Hoopes, our editorial support at the MIT Press.

Introduction: Why Classification in the Wild?

> The demand for certainty is one which is natural to man, but is nevertheless an intellectual vice. If you take your children for a picnic on a doubtful day, they will demand a dogmatic answer as to whether it will be fine or wet, and be disappointed in you when you cannot be sure.
>
> —Bertrand Russell

The desire to assign a person to a class—friend or foe, trustworthy or not—is inherent to human nature. It provides the bricks from which intelligence is built. Without forming classes, we would notice only the particular, and any general idea would be out of reach. But how do we make classifications? And how should we?

Psychologists tend to focus on well-defined situations, where all characteristics of the entities to be classified are known with certainty, including probabilities. To achieve the goal of experimental control, the typical lab experiment requires people to allocate to classes artificial objects, such as circles and triangles that vary in color and size, that is, in terms of a precisely known, fixed number of dimensions.

Classification in the Wild, in contrast, exits the certainty of the lab and looks at fundamental uncertainty. *In the wild* refers to real-world situations where, unlike in the typical psychological experiment, the future is not knowable, and uncertainty cannot be meaningfully reduced to probability.[1] Such uncertainty does not necessarily apply to all real-world situations. A player in a casino, for instance, can calculate the probabilities of winning. In the great majority of other situations, however, uncertainty prevails—be it choosing the financial products in which one should invest or the most appropriate partner to marry. Jimmie Savage, the father of modern Bayesian decision theory, argued that even planning a picnic lies outside his theory because one cannot know in advance all events that could possibly happen.[2] The relevant information may not be available in the first place or may even change from day to day. That raises the question whether classification in the wild can actually be based on science. Our answer is affirmative. This book introduces precise, *formal* models of classification that are often absent in otherwise interesting and useful work in applied psychology.[3] As we will see, these formal models combine well with the expertise of practitioners, thus the "science and art" in the book's subtitle.

Researchers in machine learning also address classification. They have developed tools such as neural networks and random forests for complex situations that go beyond the lab experiment. These tools are able to deal with complexity and uncertainty but are typically not transparent.[4] For instance, when systems based on these tools are used in financing or in courts of law, loan applicants and defendants are typically mystified about why they are classified as untrustworthy and denied a loan or bail. Often such systems fail to be transparent not only to the bank or the judge but also to the engineers who created them.

Classification in the Wild is committed to increasing transparency in situations of uncertainty. It provides tools that are easy to understand, memorize, teach, and execute. These tools allow practitioners to make fast and accurate decisions when no fancy machine learning program is at hand, as at the site of an accident or suicide attack. It also informs machine learning in how to construct transparent algorithms in the first place, rather than trying to explain opaque algorithms after the fact.

Another deep difference exists between cognitive psychology and machine learning. Psychology is mostly descriptive, answering the question of how people actually make classifications. Machine learning is prescriptive, answering the question of how one should make classifications. *Classification in the Wild* integrates the "is" and the "ought." It deals with heuristics that often are both descriptive and prescriptive; that is, they describe what experienced practitioners actually do, while also suggesting how their practices can be improved.

The classification tools we present in this book are known under the rubric of *bounded rationality*, a term coined in the 1950s by Herbert Simon,[5] one of the founders of artificial intelligence (AI) and a pioneer of the cognitive revolution. The modern study of bounded rationality in Simon's tradition is the program of *fast-and-frugal heuristics*, on which these classification tools are based.[6] Fast-and-frugal heuristics are useful additions to existing models in cognitive psychology and machine learning, allowing for fast, transparent, and accurate classifications under uncertainty.

Classification in the Wild provides points of contact where cognitive psychology and machine learning can meet. It shows how to extend the psychological study of classification to the real world of uncertainty. It also shows how to derive simple and accurate classification rules from first cognitive principles, the human abilities of *counting* and *ordering*. Additionally, the book contributes to the goal of interpretable machine learning. Fast-and-frugal classification rules can be easily understood and applied.

In *Classification in the Wild*, we make two key arguments:

Simple rules do well in the wild. In stable situations such as the games of chess and Go or face recognition, complex algorithms outperform fast-and-frugal heuristics if large amounts of data are available. In the wild, by contrast, where the future is uncertain and may differ from the past in unpredictable ways, simple heuristics can outperform complex methods regardless of whether the available data are big or small. We call this the *unstable-world principle.*

Transparency is a key value. More and more our lives are influenced by algorithms that classify citizens according to their creditworthiness, health conditions, and social and political attitudes. The underlying logic of these algorithms is often opaque, be it inherently or with the aim to protect trade secrets. Fast-and-frugal heuristics, on the other hand, are transparent by design. In sensitive domains such as health, wealth, and justice, the ability to understand algorithms is indispensable for citizens in a participatory democracy. Contrary to common wisdom in parts of machine learning, which assume that the most accurate algorithms must be inherently complicated and uninterpretable, we show that transparent algorithms are often as accurate as black-box models. We call this the *transparency-meets-accuracy principle.*

In this book, we show that these two arguments go together. The choice is not between using complex algorithms that are hard to understand and simple ones that are hardly accurate. In the wild, simplicity and transparency are not enemies of accuracy.

1 Four Cases of Classification in the Wild

At the site of a multivehicle accident, paramedics use triage systems to classify victims into those who need immediate attention, those whose treatment can be delayed, and those who have only minor injuries. Triage is an act of classification: paramedics consider classes and use a classification rule based on observable cues. These cues include whether the victim can walk, breathe, and follow simple commands. Classification brings order into the chaos of an accident site and tells paramedics whom to treat first to save as many lives as possible.

More generally, the ability to categorize individual persons or entities into groups that share relevant cues is one of the most basic forms of intelligence. Without it, our brains would be lost in a multitude of specific observations and memories. Here is a first definition:

To classify means to assign individuals to classes based on cues using a classification rule.

Classification has two common meanings: first, the act of determining a set of classes, that is, developing a taxonomy; second, the act of determining a classification rule and assigning each object to one of a given set of classes. In this book, we deal with the second meaning. These classifications can serve two goals: to make a *diagnosis* or a *prediction*. Doctors in many countries ask pregnant women to undergo an HIV test that classifies them as either HIV positive or HIV negative. A diagnosis—in this case whether a woman is infected or not—concerns an event that has already occurred. A prediction, in contrast, concerns the future: when a credit score algorithm classifies an applicant for a mortgage loan as creditworthy or not, it predicts whether the customer will repay the loan with interest in time. Diagnosis and prediction thus differ but are also closely related. The triage system, for instance, is a diagnostic system about the current health state of the victim but also contains a prediction about whether the victim will survive.

How people make classifications can be studied in psychological laboratories. In laboratory studies, the individuals are typically undergraduate students, and the classes, cues, and classification rules are defined and controlled by the experimenter. For example, individuals are asked to assign geometrical figures that vary according to a fixed number of dimensions, such as color and shape, to classes—such as assigning black triangles to class A, and white squares to class B.[1] To ensure the desired experimental control, these studies typically use artificial tasks that the participants have never encountered before. The interest lies in observing what rules participants use or how quickly they learn the optimal rule. We refer to well-defined tasks where it is possible to know the optimal classification rule as classification "in the lab."[2]

Classification, however, can also be studied "in the wild." The site of a multivehicle accident offers an example; predicting whether a potential borrower will default offers another. In general, many factors are at work in these situations, including some that can never be anticipated. Thus the relevant cues may need to be identified first. And unlike in the experimental situation designed to have an optimal classification rule, the considerable uncertainty inherent in many aspects of the real-world situation defies the ideal of optimality. Here is the important proposition:

In the wild, where the future may be different from the past in unpredictable ways, the optimal classification rule is not knowable.

In these situations, uncertainty exists about the relevant cues, the classes, or the optimal classification rule. Although finding the best rules is not possible in the wild, it is possible to find good rules and improve on existing ones. Classification in the wild can handle existing situations without having to transform them into a controlled world in the hope that the optimal rules in the lab will then generalize back to real life. In this book, we therefore leave the study of classification in the lab to the many excellent books and articles already written on the topic and focus on the study of making classifications under fundamental uncertainty in the wild.

Distinguishing between the lab and the wild is crucial for evaluating a classification rule. Useful classification rules differ systematically between both situations. In a stable, controlled world, a rule that is fine-tuned on past experience is likely to be successful. Fine-tuning tends to result in complex classification rules provided by the standard repertoire in statistics and machine learning. In the dynamic, volatile wild, by contrast, changes can occur out of the blue, and fine-tuning past experience can result in massive prediction error. Here it may be desirable to reduce rather than increase the complexity of the rule to a certain degree, which is the key principle of this book:

Simple rules do well in the wild.

A crucial advantage of simple rules is their transparency and usability. They can be easily understood, taught, remembered, and executed by users such as paramedics and doctors.

Simple rules are also known as *heuristics*. In this book, we focus on two classes of heuristics that exploit two core abilities of human intelligence: counting and ordering. The family of *tallying heuristics* simply counts reasons for assigning an individual to a class. The family of *fast-and-frugal trees* orders reasons and allows for quick decisions simply based on just one or a few of these reasons.

We begin with four illustrations of classification in the wild: predicting the next president of the United States, screening for HIV, bailing or jailing, and medical triage at the 9/11 site. The common denominator of these situations is that uncertainty abounds, albeit of different kinds and to different degrees. We may lack perfect knowledge of the cues, of the probabilities that a cue results in a correct classification, or of what the best classification rule might be. For instance, if elections were decided by playing roulette in a casino, red versus black numbers, it would be possible to calculate the accurate probabilities of who will win. Playing roulette is calculable risk, not uncertainty. Yet election polls often fail because voters do not admit to their choice, change their mind at the last moment, or stay home rather than vote because they believe their ballot will have no impact on the outcome.

Predicting the next president entails classifying presidential candidates who compete in the US presidential elections that take place every four years; the two classes are "winners" and "losers." The challenge is to identify the cues and the classification rule that assigns one of the two final candidates to the class of winners. In other words, how can one predict who will be the next president of the United States?

1.1   Keys to the White House

Prediction is very difficult, especially about the future.
—attributed to Niels Bohr (also to Mark Twain, Yogi Berra, and a host of others)

Quite a few US citizens could not believe their eyes on November 8, 2016, when they saw the results of the presidential election. The polls had predicted Hillary Clinton's victory by a large margin, the *New York Times Upshot* had predicted an 85 percent versus 15 percent chance of her winning, and, on election day, the statistician Nate Silver predicted a 71.4 percent probability for her.[3] Big data, polls, and prediction markets were confidently unanimous in their forecasts. "If you believe in Big Data analytics, it's time to begin planning for a Hillary Clinton presidency," wrote the columnist Jon Markman in *Forbes*.[4]

One notable voice, however, dissented. Allan Lichtman, distinguished professor of history at the American University, predicted that Donald Trump would win. Lichtman has an excellent track record of correctly predicting all elections since 1984, relying neither on big data nor on complex algorithms or polls. Around 1980, he developed the Keys to the White House, a forecasting system that takes a different approach. It does not deliver ostensibly precise probabilities of winning but simply predicts who will win. The system is based on a deep historical analysis of every US presidential election from 1860 to 1980, which delivered the "keys" that turn US voters' minds.

The Keys
A key is a reason that matters to US voters. There are just thirteen keys, each of which is stated as a proposition that can be categorized as either true or false. To simplify, each key is phrased so that the response "true" favors election or reelection of the candidate from the incumbent party, and "false" favors election of the candidate from the challenging party.[5]

Key 1: *Incumbent-party mandate*. After the midterm elections, the incumbent party holds more seats in the US House of Representatives than it did after the previous midterm elections.

Key 2: *Nomination contest*. There is no serious contest for the incumbent-party nomination.

Key 3: *Incumbency*. The incumbent-party candidate is the sitting president.

Key 4: *Third party*. There is no significant third-party or independent campaign.

Key 5: *Short-term economy*. The economy is not in recession during the election campaign.

Key 6: *Long-term economy*. Real annual per capita economic growth during the term equals or exceeds mean growth during the two previous terms.

Key 7: *Policy change*. The incumbent administration effects major changes in national policy.

Key 8: *Social unrest*. There is no sustained social unrest during the term.

Key 9: *Scandal*. The incumbent administration is untainted by major scandal.

Key 10: *Foreign or military failure*. The incumbent administration suffers no major failure in foreign or military affairs.

Key 11: *Foreign or military success*. The incumbent administration achieves a major success in foreign or military affairs.

Key 12: *Incumbent charisma*. The incumbent-party candidate is charismatic or a national hero.

Key 13: *Challenger charisma*. The challenging-party candidate is not charismatic or a national hero.

Note something peculiar about the keys. All of them concern the incumbent party, its past performance, and its current candidate, with the sole exception of the thirteenth key, the challenger's charisma. In 2012, when the Republican candidate Mitt Romney challenged President Barack Obama, Lichtman counted all keys as "true" except numbers 1, 6, and 12. Some of the keys, such as whether the candidate is the sitting president, require no judgment, while others, such as charisma, do. Lichtman deals with this problem by defining standards and criteria. For instance, charismatic leaders as defined by Lichtman include Franklin D. Roosevelt, Dwight D. Eisenhower, John F. Kennedy, and Barack Obama in 2008 (but not in 2012).

The Beauty of Simplicity I: Don't Weigh, Just Count

A question remains: how should these keys be combined? The methodological reflex in the statistical sciences would be to run a logistic regression across all elections to determine the optimal weighting. However, this approach might run the danger of modeling noise, given the sparse data for the few presidential elections. What makes the keys system so striking is that it uses a simple weighting scheme: all keys are given the same weight. Its underlying logic is that in situations of uncertainty, one should simply count, without trying to weigh. Counting keys is a *tallying* system; the tallying rule here is the following:

> *Keys to the White House: If six or more keys are negative (false), then the challenger will win.*

This rule is radically simple. In late September 2016, weeks before the election, Lichtman considered the keys to be "settled" and made a count. Six keys turned against Hillary Clinton, the incumbent-party candidate.[6]

Key 1: The democrats were crushed in the midterm elections.

Key 3: The sitting president was not running.

Key 4: There was a significant third-party campaign by libertarian Gary Johnson, anticipated to acquire 5 percent or more of the votes.

Key 7: There was no major policy change in Obama's second term.

Key 11: Obama did not have any smashing foreign policy successes.

Key 12: Hillary Clinton is not charismatic in comparison to, say, Franklin Roosevelt.

Because six keys were negative, the rule predicted that Donald Trump would win. This particular election was certainly not easy to predict, and a tally of six was the minimum required for an upset of the incumbent party.

There is one important caveat. According to Lichtman, the keys predict the majority vote, which Trump did not win.[7] No prediction system is perfect, however, and the predictions based on the keys system approximated the actual outcome more closely than did the polls, prediction markets, and the big data algorithms. Moreover, as mentioned before, the system's predictions have been accurate for all elections since 1984. Above all, the example illustrates that "in the wild," a simple rule can easily compete with big data analytics or surveys based on masses of data. Equally important is that the rule is transparent: one can easily understand the rule of the keys and discuss its logic, unlike big data analytics and nontransparent neural networks.

By virtue of their transparency, the keys reveal a challenging political logic that contradicts current campaign wisdom. All the keys involve the party holding the White House and its candidate, not the challenger—with the exception of the challenger's charisma key. Since 1984, this last key has been negative only once, when Barack Obama was the challenger in 2008. Otherwise the keys deal with the economy, foreign policy successes, social unrest, scandal, and policy innovation. If people fared well during the previous term, the incumbent candidate will win, otherwise lose. If the challenger wins, the reasons have little to do with him or her but solely reflect the perceived performance of the incumbent party in the previous term and its candidate.

This message is a radical one. It conflicts with the importance attributed to winning TV debates, to raising the most money, and to investing in advertising and news coverage. If the psychology underlying the keys is true, campaign managers matter little on election day, as does the concern about campaign strategies. Many people who could not believe their eyes on election day have asked what incited other US citizens to vote for Trump, who insulted women, Muslims, and the Pope, among others. If the psychology underlying the Keys to the White House is correct, then that is the wrong question. US voters did not vote for Trump; they voted against the previous governing party and its candidate. Trump essentially won for reasons that had little to do with him personally.

The Keys to the White House also shed new light on the rationality of US voters, which has been ridiculed ever since Philip Converse's seminal study on the belief systems of mass publics.[8] Many have since wondered how a democracy can function when voters know so little about the candidates and when what they know is of little relevance. For instance, it was reported that the most widely known facts about George H. W. Bush were that he hated broccoli and his dog was named Millie.[9] According to the Keys to the White House, however, voters are little swayed by anecdotes, campaign rhetoric, or TV duels and are less narrow-minded than often depicted. What they care about are the thirteen keys. If that is true, then the lesson is a different one: parties need to become more efficient and invest in solid political work.

Would the keys system also work for elections in other countries with different political systems? That question has yet to be investigated. Nonetheless, the central message could prove useful to politicians and the media in every country: to focus on governance, not on advertising and campaign tactics.

1.2   Screening for HIV

> I'll kill myself if I test positive.
>
> —a patient[10]

HIV (human immunodeficiency virus) infects vital cells in the immune system and causes HIV infection and, eventually, AIDS (acquired immuno-deficiency syndrome).[11] AIDS involves a progressive failure of the immune system. It allows life-threatening infections and cancers to thrive. An HIV infection can occur through the transfer of bodily fluids such as blood, semen, vaginal fluids, and breast milk; without treatment, the average survival after infection is about ten years.

Screening for HIV involves testing individuals who do not show any symptoms. The US Preventive Services Task Force, for instance, recommends that clinicians screen for HIV infection in all adolescents and adults aged fifteen to sixty-five years, including all pregnant women.[12] On a less voluntary basis, blood banks screen potential donors, immigration officers screen immigrants, and armed forces screen recruits and personnel on active duty. Many individuals, including professional HIV counselors, believe that the results are absolutely certain.[13] Yet no test is certain—not even the most accurate ones such as HIV tests.

A false positive occurs when the test result is positive (that is, suspicious, indicating HIV) but the person is not infected. These false alarms can have extremely destructive consequences. Cases have been documented where individuals with false-positive results committed suicide, were socially excluded, or suffered from the side effects of heavy medication treatments.[14] A second type of error is also possible: when the test result is negative although the person is in fact infected with HIV. Such misses, or false negatives, can endanger the health of others. If wrongly diagnosed as not infected, a person can unwittingly infect sexual partners.

The Beauty of Simplicity II: Don't Weigh, Just Order

To reduce errors, laboratories typically perform a sequence of tests. Practices, however, vary between laboratories and countries. Typically, a lab will first conduct an ELISA (enzyme-linked immunosorbent assay or, in short, enzyme immunoassay). For this, a drop of blood suffices. The lab reports the test result as a number, which is then transformed into a positive or negative result by using a cutoff. The setting of the cutoff is necessarily arbitrary, a matter of ongoing controversy, and one of the many uncertainties in HIV testing.

If the outcome of the first ELISA is negative, then the testing procedure stops, and the client is informed of the good news, that is, "no HIV." If, however, the result is positive, the client is not told the result. Instead a second ELISA test is typically performed, preferably from a different manufacturer.

If the second ELISA is negative, then the procedure stops, and the client is informed of having no HIV. However, if the result is positive, it is not communicated, but instead a final test, the Western blot, is applied. Like the ELISA, the Western blot is an antibody detection test. It is often called the *confirmatory* test, not because its result is certain, as some HIV counselors believe,[15] but because it leads to the final diagnosis of "HIV" or "no HIV." Figure 1.1 shows the entire testing sequence. Complications such as indeterminate Western blot tests are not included.

The classification rule for HIV status, shown in this figure, is an instance of a *fast-and-frugal tree*. It orders the three tests in a sequence. After each ELISA test, one outcome leads to an immediate diagnosis; after the last test, the Western blot, a decision is made either way.

Why are the tests conducted in this order? One reason is that the ELISA is cheaper. But there is another reason. The ELISA is applied first because it produces fewer *misses* than the Western blot. That is, when the ELISA is negative, it is less often wrong. In other words, the ELISA has a high *sensitivity*, which is defined as the proportion of people who test positive among those who are infected. Its high sensitivity is crucial because the exit for the ELISA is "no HIV," meaning that the only error this diagnosis can make is a miss. Similarly, the second ELISA is also associated with the same exit. The Western blot, in contrast, produces fewer false positives than the ELISA. In other words, the Western blot has a high *specificity*, which is defined as the proportion of people who test negative among those who are not infected. The Western blot is the only test that can lead to the diagnosis "HIV." To summarize, the reason for the order and the exits is that ELISA is more sensitive and the Western blot is more specific.

At this point, it is useful to introduce more general terminology than that for the specific case of HIV screening. Throughout the book, we will use the general term *cues* for ELISA tests, Lichtman's keys, or other attributes.

We will use the symbol k for the number of cues; here $k = 3$. A cue is called a *binary* cue if it has only two values, such as positive and negative, or yes and no. The spaces in a fast-and-frugal tree where a classification can be made are called *exits*. In a tree, exits are designated by circles, and cues by rectangles. For k binary cues, a fast-and-frugal tree has exactly $k + 1$ exits. For instance, in figure 1.1, we see four exits, three of which lead to the diagnosis "no HIV" and one to "HIV." If, by contrast, the classification rule was a full decision tree, then every person would undergo all three tests, and a decision would be made on the basis of all three results. A full tree with k binary cues has 2^k exits; in the case of HIV testing, this would require eight exits instead of four. A fast-and-frugal tree simplifies the classification process in several respects, including the use of fewer cues and exits, as well as no weighting and adding of cue values.

Why a Fast-and-Frugal Tree instead of a Full Tree?
Using a full tree to screen for HIV would require more tests and generate more data, which one might presume is always more beneficial. Surprisingly, that

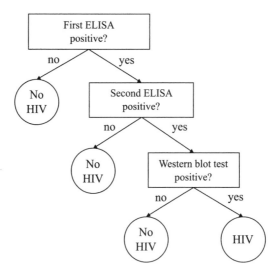

Figure 1.1
Screening for HIV in the general public. If the first enzyme immunoassay (ELISA) is negative, the diagnosis is "no HIV." Otherwise a second ELISA is performed; if it is negative, the diagnosis is "no HIV." Otherwise a Western blot test is performed, which determines the final classification.

is not the case. To better understand this counterintuitive answer, consider 10 million low-risk individuals who are screened for HIV. Let us assume that one in every ten thousand of them has undetected HIV, which is a realistic estimate for many countries. Thus, among the 10 million, we expect one thousand people who are infected without knowing it. A perfect test would classify everyone who is infected with HIV as positive and everyone who is not as negative. But no test in existence can attain such perfection.

According to a large study, a single ELISA has a sensitivity of around 99.7 percent and a specificity of about 98.5 percent, although values vary considerably.[16] A sensitivity of 99.7 percent means that out of 1,000 infected individuals, we expect the first ELISA to correctly identify 997 as positive while missing 3. That is, when the fast-and-frugal tree in figure 1.1 is applied to 10 million people, all but three classifications at the first exit, "no HIV," are expected to be correct. Continuing to test everyone at this exit with a second ELISA and the more expensive Western blot could thus correct only three misses at most.

Using a full tree would not only be utterly expensive in terms of time and budget spent but also generate new errors, namely, new false alarms. Consider again the first exit of the fast-and-frugal tree. At this exit, we expect that 98.5 percent (which is the specificity of the ELISA) of the 9,999,000 healthy individuals will correctly be classified as "no HIV." This amounts to 9,849,015 correct classifications (and three incorrect ones, as mentioned before). If we continued testing all these individuals, the second ELISA would likely eliminate the three misses but create many more new false positives.[17]

The general point is that running more tests may eliminate a few misses but lead to many false alarms. At the same time, the numbers used are far from being as precise as they appear. In fact, great uncertainty prevails about the actual sensitivity and specificity of the ELISA and the Western blot, and the reported values vary considerably between studies and laboratories, with a range of 97 percent to 99.999 percent.[18] If we applied those numbers to the earlier example, then, we would expect not three but something between zero and thirty misses, with an unknown probability distribution. The source of this uncertainty is manifold: we have no universally agreed-on procedure to determine what a positive or negative result is, meaning that procedures vary among labs and clinics; the tests themselves are produced by different manufacturers and thus vary in quality; results not only are positive or negative but can also be indeterminate; and no reliable data about the dependencies between subsequent tests exist for us to estimate the conditional sensitivities and specificities.

HIV testing illustrates diagnostic situations in which we can expect fast-and-frugal trees to be highly efficient. If one class (such as HIV infection in the general population) is rare and the other frequent (no infection), choosing a fast-and-frugal tree over a full tree can (1) considerably reduce physicians' time spent with testing, as well as the financial burden to health-care spending, and (2) protect large numbers of individuals from being falsely diagnosed at the cost of relatively few misses. Thus a full tree is not dominant over a fast-and-frugal tree. The general lesson is that more tests are not always better.

The Keys to the White House and the HIV testing procedure share a common philosophy. Both simplify, are easily comprehensible, and can compete strongly with or even outperform more elaborate and time-consuming procedures. What they differ in is how they simplify. The Keys to the White House system uses a relatively large number of cues (the thirteen keys), treats all as equal, and simply makes a count, a tally. The HIV testing procedure relies on a relatively small number of cues (one, two, or three tests) but orders them in a sequence. In neither case are cues weighted quantitatively or the dependencies between cues estimated. Tallying and fast-and-frugal trees are two different ways to create robust classification rules.

1.3   To Bail or Jail?

> We have magistrates who are dinner-ladies and scientists, bus drivers and teachers, plumbers and housewives. They have different faiths and come from different ethnic backgrounds, some have disabilities. All are serving their communities, ensuring that local justice is dispensed by local people.
> —Lord Irvine, Labour Lord Chancellor

There exists an ancient ideal that local justice should be served by local people. The legal system of England and Wales has a long history of involving the local community in dealing with criminal cases such as theft, damage, sexual assault, and dangerous driving. The local volunteers are known as magistrates, or justices of the peace. Most are laypeople who are not paid for their service, apart from an allowance to compensate loss of earnings and transportation costs. Magistrates sit in court for a half day every one or two weeks, in a bench of two or three. Their task is to determine whether a defendant should be allowed to "go free" until the next hearing of the case, that is, be granted bail (unconditional release) or else denied it, resulting in either jail or bail with conditions such as curfew. Reasons for denying bail include suspicion that the defendant might commit another crime, threaten witnesses, or leave the country before the trial. Magistrates' decisions can have significant consequences for individual defendants, but also for the public. Compared to individuals who are bailed, remanded defendants are more likely to lose their homes, jobs, and family ties.[19] At the same time, bailing a defendant who subsequently commits another crime poses a danger to society at large.

How should magistrates make such consequential decisions? The law says that magistrates should pay regard to the nature and seriousness of the offense; to the character, community ties, and bail record of the defendant; and to the strength of the prosecution's case, the likely sentence if convicted, and any other factor that appears to be relevant.[20] The legal ideal of due process is based on a thorough analysis of the characteristics of each individual defendant to minimize the number of innocent defenders who are treated punitively. However, the law is mute on how magistrates should combine all these pieces of information. Nor do magistrates have the opportunity to learn from experience; the legal system provides no feedback on whether magistrates' decisions were in fact appropriate or not. In addition, magistrates are faced with further sources of uncertainty. They often lack information, and even if information is available, magistrates do not know how useful it is in predicting whether a defendant will abscond or interfere with witnesses if bailed. Above all, magistrates work under daily time pressure due to the high caseload. In England and Wales alone, magistrates have to deal with some two million defendants every year, that is, the majority of all criminal cases.

How Do Magistrates Decide?

In interviews, magistrates tend to report that they properly examine all the evidence to treat individuals fairly and without bias. For instance, one explained that the decision "depends on an enormous weight of balancing information, together with our experience and training," and another that "each case is an individual case." The chairman of a council stated, "We are trained to question, and to assess carefully the evidence we are given."[21] Basically, their statements echo what the law expects from them. One magistrate declared, "You can't study magistrates' complex decision making."[22]

The psychologist Mandeep Dhami observed several hundred hearings in two London courts over a four-month period to identify the rationale that underlies magistrates' actions.[23] The average time a bench spent with each defendant was between six and ten minutes. The cues available to the London magistrates included the defendants' age, race, gender, strength of community ties, seriousness of offense, kind of offense, number of offenses, relation to the victim, plea (guilty, not guilty, no plea), previous convictions, bail record, the strength of the prosecution's case, maximum penalty if convicted, circumstances of adjournment, length of adjournment, number of previous adjournments, prosecution request, defense request, previous court bail decisions, and police bail decision. However, the actual information available changed from case to case. The magistrates also saw whether the defendant was present at the bail hearing, whether or not he or she was legally represented, and by whom.

Dhami recorded the information available for each case and tested how well a linear adding and weighting of all these cues could predict the bail decisions compared with fast-and-frugal trees that considered only a few cues. The fast-and-frugal trees predicted the decisions in both courts best. Figure 1.2 shows the tree that modeled magistrates' decision making in the first court. It predicted 92 percent of all decisions correctly. The decisions are called "bail" and "jail" in figure 1.2, where "jail" is short for punitive conditions, including jail and curfew. Its logic is simple: When the prosecution opposed bail or requested conditional bail, the magistrates also opposed bail. If not, or if no information was available, a second cue came into play. If a previous court had imposed conditions or remand in custody, the magistrates also decided not to bail. Otherwise they considered a third cue and based their decisions on whether the police had imposed conditions. The fast-and-frugal tree that predicted the magistrates' decision in the second court had exactly the same structure; moreover, two of the three cues were identical.[24]

We can observe a striking divide between what magistrates reported they did and what the classification rule in figure 1.2 indicates they did. As mentioned before, magistrates, when asked, tended to say that they carefully

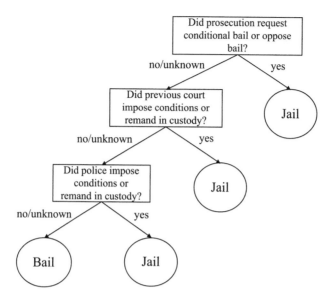

Figure 1.2
To bail or jail? A fast-and-frugal tree describing how London magistrates decided whether to grant a defendant bail or else deny bail. Denying bail can mean either jail or imposing punitive conditions such as curfew, for short "jail."

weighted all the evidence. Few of them mentioned the three cues in the bail tree. A second study with a different group of London magistrates confirmed the result. Although magistrates relied on only a few cues, they often requested more information concerning the defendant, which the magistrates subsequently ignored in making their decisions.[25] Other independent research confirmed the specific cues in figure 1.2: magistrates followed the bail recommendations of the police in 99 percent of the cases and agreed with the prosecution's request 95 percent of the time.[26]

To understand this divide, one needs to understand the magistrates' psychological situation. Their official task is to do justice to each defendant and the public, which means to balance the likelihood of the two possible errors. These are the same errors that HIV tests can make: misses and false alarms. A miss occurs when a suspect is released on bail and subsequently commits another crime, threatens a witness, or does not turn up in court. A false alarm occurs when a suspect is imprisoned who would not have committed any of these offenses. Yet magistrates do not have the necessary information to calculate the best balance between the two error rates. They do not know the frequency of these errors, nor does the law give them any instructions. For one, the English legal institutions do not collect statistics about the error rates in magistrates' decisions. And even if statistics were kept about how often misses occur, it would be impossible to do the same for false alarms; no method can determine whether jailed individuals would have committed a crime had they been bailed. That is, the magistrates operate under considerable uncertainty and without knowing how to solve their task.

In this situation, magistrates apparently instead try to solve a task they are more capable of: to protect themselves first. This motivation is called *defensive decision making*.[27] Magistrates can be proved wrong only if a suspect who was released fails to appear in court or commits an offense or crime while on bail—the cases that often make the headlines. To protect themselves against potential accusations by the media or the victims, magistrates follow the defensive logic embodied in the fast-and-frugal tree in figure 1.2, where every exit except one is "jail." They grant bail only if neither the prosecution nor a previous court nor the police had imposed or requested a punitive decision such as imprisonment. Thus, if they mistakenly bailed a defendant, the magistrates can defend themselves by claiming that the offense was not foreseeable. This form of defensive decision making is also known as "passing the buck."

The bail-or-jail tree in figure 1.2 is descriptive: it models how magistrates actually make their classifications. It is not prescriptive; that is, it does not offer a procedure for how magistrates should make the bail-or-jail decision. By contrast, the legal concept of due process is prescriptive but, as noted, does not specify a classification rule. Due process, however, appears to be violated by this classification rule shown in figure 1.2: magistrates paid little attention to the individual defendant and instead relied on what the police, prosecution, or a previous court requested. One could argue that magistrates simply used a shortcut after the police or prosecution had already examined all the evidence concerning the defendant. However, the three defensive cues in the fast-and-frugal tree were not correlated with other cues such as the nature and seriousness of the offense.[28] Moreover, if that argument were true, it would raise the question of why the institution of magistrates is needed in the first place.

The bail-or-jail tree is transparent: one can easily see the defensive logic of the bail decisions and its conflict with due process. In US courts, however, judges, probation officers, and parole officers are increasingly using complex predictive algorithms often based on big data and machine learning, which lack transparency. These complex algorithms supposedly classify more accurately and with less bias than humans do. Since 1998 the COMPAS risk assessment tool has been used to assess more than 1 million offenders. The algorithm predicts a defendant's probability of committing a misdemeanor or felony within the next two years, based on 137 features and the defendant's past criminal record. For instance, a Wisconsin man was sentenced to six years in prison based in part on the COMPAS algorithm that predicted for him a high probability of reoffense (recidivism) and violence. Neither the judges nor the defendant could possibly have understood how the algorithm works, given that it is a trade secret. When the quality of these predictions was finally tested, it turned out that using only two cues—the defendant's age and number of previous convictions—proved to be about as good as the COMPAS algorithm with over 137 cues. Moreover, an analysis of one thousand defendants revealed that COMPAS made errors (false alarms and misses together) in about 35 percent of the cases, which is as many as laypeople make who have no experience in predicting recidivism.[29] In addition, ProPublica reported that the algorithm showed a bias against African Americans.[30] We know of no data on how well experienced magistrates perform, but it would be difficult to commit more errors than those occurring with the "black-box" algorithm for prediction.

The study of the London courts caused quite a stir after it was published. How desirable is a legal system in which magistrates mainly "pass the buck"? Given that the bail tree predicts over 90 percent of all bail decisions made, should the ideal of local people serving local justice be replaced with an algorithm such as the fast-and-frugal tree in figure 1.2? Another, more constructive solution would be for the legal system to support magistrates and enable them to make less defensive and more informed decisions.

1.4 Emergency Treatment at Ground Zero

At the end of the day, you need a very simple tool that says that a patient is a priority.

—Colin Smart, creator of the SMART Triage Tag

On the morning of September 11, 2001, Louis Cook of the Emergency Medical Services division of the New York City Fire Department was told that an aircraft had struck the World Trade Center. He recalled first assuming that a light aircraft had gone astray from its air corridor.[31] When he and his paramedics arrived at the site, they were asked to set up a triage area in Tower 1, which had just been hit, on a floor below the fire. But before the paramedics could achieve much, a second aircraft hit Tower 2, which soon collapsed. After Tower 1 also collapsed, the emergency services experienced havoc, resulting in immense loss of lives among the rescue teams. Before the dust of the twin collapse had settled, the remaining teams entered the chaos of the collapse zone and used a triage system to help identify victims who needed help first. The system is called Simple Triage and Rapid Treatment (START).[32] START classifies injured victims into four classes: those who need *immediate* treatment, those with serious injuries but whose treatment can be *delayed*, those with *minor* injuries, and those who are *dying* and can only be given palliative care and pain relief (fig. 1.3).

The first question is whether the person can walk. If yes, the classification is "minor." If not, the next question is whether the person is breathing. If not, the classification is "dying." If, however, paramedics can clear the victim's airway by tilting the head so that breathing is possible, this leads to "immediate" treatment. If the person can breathe without help, there are three further questions where a "no" always leads to immediate treatment. Only if all these questions are answered "yes" is treatment "delayed."

In the chaos of an event with mass casualties, the rescuer marks the victim after classification with a tag whose color reflects the class, that is, the severity, of the injury. A green tag signifies "minor" status, a yellow tag "delayed" status, a red tag "immediate" status, and a black tag "dying" or "dead." Tagging the victims makes the diagnosis visible to other rescue personnel and prevents unnecessarily repeating the triage process in the chaos of a terrorist attack or a mass accident.

START is a fast-and-frugal tree with four classes, unlike the previous examples that have two classes. It also deviates from the previous trees in that one of its questions—about breathing—has three possible answers, where two answers directly lead to a classification. As its name indicates, START is simple and rapid.

START was developed in 1983 by members of Hoag Hospital in Newport Beach, California, and is widely used today in the United States and

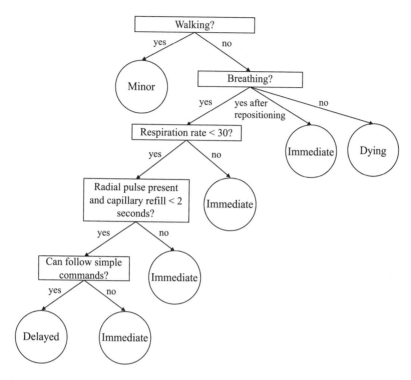

Figure 1.3

Simple Triage and Rapid Treatment (START), a classification system for identifying victims who need help immediately.

Europe. Several modifications with varying numbers of classes and cues exist, including JumpSTART for children under eight years old.[33] START helps responders make classifications under conditions of high uncertainty. Using this tree, paramedics need not search and integrate all relevant information to reach a classification. Rather, in emergency situations, they are equipped with rules that are simple: easily taught, easily remembered, and quickly executed.

1.5 In the Lab and in the Wild

The tallying of Keys to the White House and the fast-and-frugal trees for HIV screening, bail decisions, and emergency treatment illustrate three general features of classification in the wild.

Uncertainty

The study of classification addresses two kinds of situations. Classification in the lab deals with well-defined situations in which the cues, their weights, and the optimal classification rule are known because the experimenter typically has created a controlled, artificial world. The rule may be deterministic or probabilistic. A rule such as "if the object is a square, black, and striped, then it belongs to class A, otherwise to class B," is deterministic if it leads to a correct classification with certainty. A rule is probabilistic if it does so with a known probability, say 90 percent.

By contrast, classification in the wild deals with real-world situations in which this degree of certainty, be it deterministic or probabilistic, is unattainable. Uncertainty arises from several sources, including the following:

Uncertainty about the cues: Unlike in the typical lab study where objects vary on a fixed, known set of cues, the set of relevant cues may not be known or knowable.

Uncertainty about the cue weights: The weights of the cues may not be known or knowable.

Uncertainty about the optimal classification rule: Under uncertainty, the optimal classification rule cannot be known.

In general, uncertainty arises in situations where the future may differ from the past in unpredictable ways. Therefore, constructing an "optimal" classification rule that describes past classifications as accurately as possible can generate error. In contrast, we argue that simple heuristics such as tallying and fast-and-frugal trees can perform well in the wild because they reduce error by relying on robust principles such as counting and ordering.

The distinction between classification in the lab and in the wild is not a categorical one; situations have higher or lower degrees of uncertainty. This distinction is reminiscent of the one made by the economist Frank Knight between *risk* and *uncertainty*, that is, between situations where the full state space of alternatives, consequences, and their probabilities is known and not known, respectively.[34] It is also reminiscent of the distinction between *known unknowns* and *unknown unknowns* in the NASA terminology popularized by former US secretary of defense Donald Rumsfeld.

Description and Prescription

A rule can be descriptive or prescriptive. It can describe *what* people do, or prescribe what they *ought* to do. Entire disciplines are divided along this boundary line: anthropology is descriptive, whereas philosophy is prescriptive; cognitive psychology is curious about how people actually make classifications, whereas machine learning is mainly interested in how classifications ought to be made. Among philosophers, a majority reject the use of psychology to inform normative theories of rationality or morality, referring to that approach as the "naturalistic fallacy," while others argue that psychology would make philosophy more realistic and relevant.[35] In behavioral economics and decision theory, normative theories of rationality (what the ideal person would do) are often proposed with scant regard for how people actually make decisions, and people's deviating behavior is then dismissed as a flaw in the human mind rather than in the normative theory itself.[36] This division between "is" and "ought" is deeply ingrained, thereby hindering interdisciplinarity.

Classification in the wild, in contrast, is both a descriptive and prescriptive research program. It defies the tradition of dividing up the sciences into the two territories of "is" and "ought." The program is to study how successful experts actually make classifications, and then investigate whether these rules are robust enough to be considered prescriptive rules. Consider HIV screening and the 9/11 triage rule. The fast-and-frugal tree in figure 1.1 describes how a majority of physicians classify people into HIV-positive and HIV-negative groups, while also serving as a prescriptive rule for how to make this classification. Similarly, the triage rule in figure 1.3 prescribes to paramedics how they ought to classify victims of an accident, while also describing how they actually proceed.

The term *description* has been used in two different ways: for describing the process or the outcome. Classification in the wild aims at models of the actual process of classification, that is, of the cognitive and behavioral steps involved. For instance, a fast-and-frugal tree describes which cue to look up first, when to stop searching for cues, and how to make a final classification. Process models differ from outcome models that aim at describing not the process but solely the final classification. As we will see in chapter 5, even some theories in cognitive psychology appear to be concerned more with the outcome than with the process.

The term *prescriptive* should not be confused with *optimal*. A classification rule is optimal only conditional to a set of assumptions. The validity of these assumptions can be guaranteed and verified in the lab but rarely in the wild. In the wild, one can find rules that are *better* than existing ones, as measured by criteria such as time to execute, ease to memorize, cost, and sensitivity and specificity, as estimated from the available data. In the wild, attempts to determine the optimal classification rule amount to wishful thinking: uncertainty (as opposed to risk) cannot be tamed by probability theory. The unstable-world principle suggests that the lab's quest for optimality should be replaced in the wild by a quest for simplicity.

Classification in the wild often starts by analyzing what successful experts actually do, and then proceeds to investigate and test these procedures as potentially prescriptive rules. Here, "is" provides ideas for "ought." This approach differs from research programs in which "ought" is defined a priori by a convenient statistical tradition, such as regression modeling and Bayesian statistics, which may have little to do with the process of how classifications are actually made.

Transparency

The focus on process delivers an important advantage: prescriptions are made transparent and can easily be taught, learned, and applied. Classification in the wild aims at transparent rules that are usable. Here is a definition:

A rule is transparent to a group of users if they can understand, memorize, teach, and execute it.

Transparency is a relative concept: a rule can be transparent for those who designed it but not for those who have to use it. Simple heuristics support transparency for all users. In contrast, a logistic regression would be far from transparent for most physicians and paramedics, and the workings of a neural network may not be transparent even to its designer. Transparency enables users to make appropriate adjustments if necessary to the classification rule in the time available and at natural locations such as in a court or at the site of an accident. For instance, if a victim is in a wheelchair, the first question of START would be omitted.

Transparency is a value that can be as important as predictive accuracy. Yet it plays only a small role in many laboratory studies in cognitive psychology, where highly complex and opaque stochastic models are proposed for relatively simple tasks. Increasing mathematical sophistication to acquire an iota of higher accuracy, which may or may not transfer to the real world, should not be a value per se.

Transparency also has legal and ethical value. In the world of big data, algorithms increasingly evaluate citizens in various respects, from their financial creditworthiness to their social credit score. At the same time, people in many countries cannot find out how their credit score is calculated and thus why a loan application was denied. Many algorithms that so strongly influence our lives are trade secrets.

The General Data Protection Regulation of the European Union that took effect in 2018 has made a legal move toward greater transparency of algorithms and the data used. It requires companies to provide customers transparent, intelligible, and easily accessible information about the use of their personal data. For automated classifications and profiling, citizens have been accorded the right to access "meaningful information about the logic involved."[37] As this book goes to press, the United States has no comparable regulation for criminal profiling, as illustrated by the use of the COMPAS algorithms for assessing the probability of recidivism, whose logic neither the judge nor the defendant (nor, presumably, the plaintiff) can understand. We believe that transparency of the algorithms that lead to personally sensitive decisions should be a citizen's right in every democracy.[38]

2 Fast-and-Frugal Classification

Simplicity is the ultimate sophistication.
—Leonardo da Vinci

In chapter 1, we discussed four cases of classification in the wild, using two families of fast-and-frugal classification: tallying and fast-and-frugal trees. We now describe these two families in detail. Serving as an illustrative example is a challenge encountered by physicians in the emergency room.

2.1 Is the Patient Having a Heart Attack?

A patient is rushed to a rural hospital in Michigan because of intense chest pain. The physician in charge needs to assign the patient either to the coronary care unit or to a regular nursing bed (with telemetry). The coronary care unit has only a limited number of beds. Furthermore, staying in it increases the patient's risk of infection. On the other hand, a regular nursing bed may not adequately cover the patient's needs if it is a case of acute ischemic heart disease, for example, if the patient is having a heart attack.

Under what conditions should physicians assign patients to the coronary care unit? In a study published in the *New England Journal of Medicine*, physicians identified seven cues that are useful in making this decision:

Pain is reported in chest or left arm.
Patient reports pressure, pain, or discomfort in chest as the most important symptom.
History of heart attack is known.
History of nitroglycerin use for chest pain is known.

Electrocardiogram shows ST segment (section between the end of the S wave
and the beginning of the T wave) with elevation or depression of 1 mm or
more.

Electrocardiogram shows ST segment abnormally "straightened" or "barred"
(but not depressed by more than 0.5 mm).

Electrocardiogram shows T waves with peaking or inversion of at least 1 mm.[1]

Notice that all seven cues can take on only two possible values, *present* or
absent. The authors of the study selected these seven from among fifty-nine
candidate cues based on various types of information that may be available
to the physician, including clinical presentation, physical findings, electrocardiogram, risk factors for coronary disease, history, and sociodemo-
graphic factors. The study used patient data collected in six hospitals in
New England.

Like the four cases discussed in chapter 1, allocating patients to the coronary care unit is a problem of classification in the wild. When encountering
the patient, the physician has access to an extremely large number of cues
that are potentially informative. Although studies have reduced this large
collection of available information to a relatively small number of diagnostic cues, we must keep in mind that these studies used data collected in a
particular geographic region at a particular time. Their conclusions do not
necessarily transfer to the patient that our physician in Michigan is facing.
The physician's problem is one of *out-of-population* prediction, where one
cannot be sure whether the classification rule developed in one population
applies elsewhere. This is a fundamental challenge for classification in the
wild. It differs from *out-of-sample* prediction, where the classification rule is
developed based on one part of the population called a *sample*, and then
tested on a different sample from the same population.

2.2 Classification

In chapter 1, we gave a preliminary definition of the classification problem. We now introduce technical terms. A classification problem asks us to
assign an instance to one of two or more possible classes, given a number
of cues. We use *instance* as an umbrella term to refer to a person, situation,
object, or any other entity to be classified. The *cue profile* refers to the vector
of cue values associated with an instance.

In many classification problems in the wild, cues often take on one of two possible values. These are called *binary* cues. For example, a symptom may be present or absent, a statement may be true or false, or the level of a given substance may be within or outside the normal range. More generally, a *categorical* cue can have two or more discrete values. For example, color may be green, amber, or red. Alternatively, a cue can have a numerical value, such as a value between zero and ten.

The coronary care problem has two classes: *regular nursing bed* and *coronary care unit*. In the wild, problems with exactly two classes are prevalent. These are called *binary classification* problems. Examples include three of the four problems introduced in chapter 1: predicting the outcome of US presidential elections, HIV testing, and bail-or-jail decisions. Our fourth example, Simple Triage and Rapid Treatment (START), allocates people to one of four classes.

Table 2.1 shows the classes and the cues of the coronary care problem. For ease of reference, the table introduces cue names in place of the longer descriptions provided earlier. In addition, it shows numeric values for cues and classes. For example, regular nursing bed and coronary care unit are represented by the numbers 0 and 1, respectively. This numerical

Table 2.1

Classes and cues of the coronary care problem

Classes	
Regular nursing bed (0)	
Coronary care unit (1)	

Cues	Possible Values
Chest pain	Absent (0), Present (1)
Chief complaint	Absent (0), Present (1)
History	Absent (0), Present (1)
Nitroglycerin	Absent (0), Present (1)
ST-change	Absent (0), Present (1)
ST-barring	Absent (0), Present (1)
T peak/inversion	Absent (0), Present (1)

representation will be useful when discussing algorithms for fast-and-frugal classification.

In machine learning, classification rules are also called *classifiers*. We use these terms interchangeably.

2.3   Fast-and-Frugal Classification

The defining characteristic of fast-and-frugal classification is simplicity. It is achieved in two ways. First, a relatively small number of cues are used to make a classification. Second, cues are combined in simple ways. As a consequence, classifications are made quickly, and it is easy to understand and explain the reasoning behind the classification. In all four case studies discussed in the previous chapter, the reasoning is fast and transparent.

What does it mean to combine the cues in simple ways? In this book, we examine two canonical approaches, both of which were inspired by psychological studies of how experts make decisions in the wild. The first approach, called *tallying*, uses cues simultaneously, giving them equal weight. The second approach, called *fast-and-frugal trees*, uses cues sequentially, one at a time, imposing a priority ordering on the cues.

Tallying

Tallying counts reasons in favor of a particular class. If the total count is above a specified threshold, the instance is assigned to that class. One example of tallying is the Keys to the White House. The system counts reasons that favor the challenger against the incumbent. If it identifies at least six such reasons, the classifier predicts that the challenger will win. Another example is a tallying rule developed by practicing physicians for the coronary care problem.[2]

Tallying for Coronary Care: If three or more cues listed in table 2.1 are present, assign the patient to the coronary care unit. Otherwise assign the patient to a regular nursing bed.

A tallying rule is specified by its target, a threshold, and reasons. These are collectively called the *parameters* of the tallying rule. The values of these parameters in Tallying for Coronary Care are shown in table 2.2.

Target: The target is the class for which reasons are counted. Tallying for Coronary Care counts how many reasons there are for assigning the

Table 2.2

Tallying for Coronary Care

Target:	Coronary care unit
Threshold:	3
Reasons:	Chest pain is present.
	Chief complaint is present.
	History is present.
	Nitroglycerin is present.
	ST-change is present.
	ST-barring is present.
	T peak/inversion is present.

patient to the coronary care unit. Thus its target is the coronary care unit. The Keys to the White House system counts how many reasons there are for predicting a win for the challenger. Thus its target is victory for the challenger.

Threshold: The threshold is the minimum number of reasons needed to assign an instance to the target class. The threshold is three in Tallying for Coronary Care and six in the Keys to the White House.

Reasons: A reason consists of one or more values of a particular cue that are indicators for the target class. Each of the thirteen keys to the White House is a reason. Tallying for Coronary Care has seven reasons, one of which is "presence of chest pain." These are examples of reasons that specify a single value for a binary cue. For categorical cues with more than two categories or numerical cues, a reason can include more than one value. For example, a reason may state that color is green or amber but not red, or that respiration rate is higher than thirty breaths per minute. Ideally, each reason uses only one cue, and each cue is used for at most one reason. These guidelines keep tallying classifiers fast and frugal. A fast-and-frugal classifier may, however, be more transparent if several cues are combined into a single reason. We leave this possibility open to the judgment of the designer. This is one of the reasons why we speak of both the science *and* the art of fast-and-frugal classification.

Consider the cue profiles of two patients shown in table 2.3. Alice has chest pain and reports it as the main symptom. Adam also has these two

Table 2.3

Cue profiles of two patients admitted to the hospital

Cue	Alice	Adam
Chest pain	Present	Present
Chief complaint	Present	Present
History	Absent	Absent
Nitroglycerin	Absent	Absent
ST-change	Absent	Present
ST-barring	Absent	Absent
T peak/inversion	Absent	Absent

Tallying for Coronary Care assigns Alice to a regular nursing bed, Adam to the coronary care unit.

cues present and additionally shows elevated ST in the cardiogram. Tallying for Coronary Care assigns Alice to a regular nursing bed because the number of reasons that are satisfied does not reach the threshold of three. In the case of Adam, the threshold is reached, and he is assigned to the coronary care unit.

In summary, tallying examines whether there are enough reasons for assigning the instance to the target class. It counts. For certain types of problems, counting is appropriate. Other types of problems require an alternative approach: ordering. We next describe a fast-and-frugal classifier that takes this alternative approach.

Fast-and-Frugal Trees

Fast-and-frugal trees examine the reasons one at a time, in a given order. Any reason, on its own, can lead directly to a classification. Figure 2.1 shows a fast-and-frugal tree created by the same physicians who developed Tallying for Coronary Care.[3]

Fast-and-Frugal Tree for Coronary Care

1. If the ST segment is depressed or elevated, assign the patient to the coronary care unit. Otherwise continue.
2. Check whether or not the patient reports chest pressure, pain, or discomfort as the most important symptom. If the answer is no, assign the patient to a regular nursing bed. Otherwise continue.

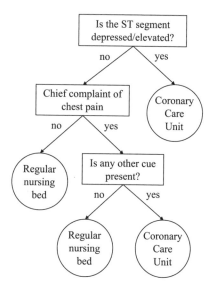

Figure 2.1
Fast-and-Frugal Tree for Coronary Care. In the third level, "any other cue" refers to history, nitroglycerin, ST-barring, and T peak/inversion.

3. Check whether any of the following cues are present: history, nitroglycerin, ST-barring, T peak/inversion. If the answer is yes, assign the patient
   to the coronary care unit. Otherwise assign the patient to a regular nursing bed.

Consider again the two patients whose cue profiles are shown in table
2.3. With Alice, the classifier follows all three steps, eventually assigning
her to a regular nursing bed. The process of classifying Adam ends much
earlier. He is assigned to the coronary care unit at the very first layer of the
tree, without the need to check any other cue. The classification of Adam is
said to be more frugal than that of Alice. Specifically, *frugality* is defined as
the number of cues that are checked to make a classification. Frugality can
be computed for a single instance or for a set of instances.

In the visual representation of the fast-and-frugal tree in figure 2.1, the
rectangles contain questions. Each of these questions checks whether a reason holds for classifying in a particular way. The circles contain the classes
to which an instance can be assigned. The lines extending from each rectangle are *branches*. They lead an instance either to a classification or to

another question. An *exit* is a branch that leads to a classification. The first question is the *root* of the tree. Any given instance is classified by starting from the root and following a path to one of the exits, answering the questions in accordance with the cue profile of the instance. We focus on trees that have exactly two branches after each question. The following definition applies to binary classifications with binary cues.

Fast-and-frugal tree: A fast-and-frugal tree has one exit at every question except for the last question, which has two exits. A fast-and-frugal tree with k questions (cues) therefore has $k + 1$ exits.

Now consider the *full tree* shown in figure 2.2. The full tree starts with the same root as that of the fast-and-frugal tree. Here, however, neither answer leads to an exit but instead leads to a second question. Each branch from the second question then leads to a third question. Only after the third question is asked and answered does the full tree make a classification.

The fast-and-frugal structure keeps the tree small and transparent. As mentioned in chapter 1, a full tree has 2^k exits, while a fast-and-frugal tree has only $k + 1$ exits. As k increases, this discrepancy grows rapidly. For instance, with 10 cues, a full tree has 1,024 exits, and a fast-and-frugal tree only 11 exits.

You may have noticed that the full tree shown in figure 2.2 makes classifications that are identical to those of the Fast-and-Frugal Tree for Coronary Care. This is not always the case because full trees are more flexible than fast-and-frugal trees. Full trees can specify classification rules that cannot be represented as fast-and-frugal trees. In contrast, a fast-and-frugal tree can always be represented as a full tree.

You may also have noticed that the exit labels at the very bottom of the full tree, when read from left to right, start with regular nursing bed and then switch to coronary care unit. This is not a coincidence. It is a property of every fast-and-frugal tree with binary cues, which we discuss in more detail in chapter 3.

Fast-and-frugal trees are made of the same building block as that of tallying: a reason for classifying the instance in a particular way, for example, for classifying a patient as HIV negative. But the use of this basic building block differs between fast-and-frugal trees and tallying. While tallying considers all reasons to be equally important, fast-and-frugal trees impose a priority ordering on them.

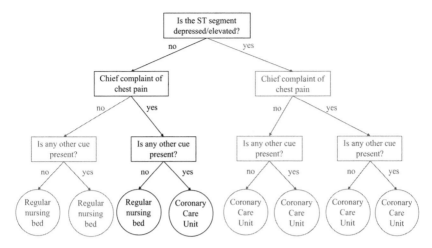

Figure 2.2
A full decision tree that makes classifications identical to those of the Fast-and-Frugal Tree for Coronary Care (fig. 2.1). The fast-and-frugal tree is embedded in the full tree and is shown in darker ink.

How can one define a fast-and-frugal tree for a given classification problem? What are the parameters of this classification rule? A fast-and-frugal tree is specified by its reasons, their exits, and their order.

Reasons: A reason is a cue, along with one or more specific values the cue may take that lead immediately to a classification. For example, the Fast-and-Frugal Tree for Coronary Care uses "chief complaint is absent" as a reason for immediately sending the patient to a nursing bed without looking up any further information. In Simple Triage and Rapid Treatment (START), a "respiration rate of 30 or more breaths per minute" is a reason for classifying the victim as needing immediate attention. In the visual representation of the tree, a reason is a rectangle, and a branch from this rectangle leads directly to an exit.

Exits: Each reason leads to one or more exits. Each exit is a classification. With binary cues, each layer of the tree has exactly one exit, except the bottom layer, which has two exits. The bottom layer of the tree leads to exits only.

Order: This is the order in which reasons are examined, beginning at the root of the tree.

In summary, a fast-and-frugal tree describes a sequential process in which reasons are checked one after another until a reason is found for making a classification. A fast-and-frugal tree deliberately ignores some of the available information.

2.4   Measuring Classifier Performance

We have described two possible classifiers for the coronary care problem: tallying and fast-and-frugal trees. Which classifier is better suited to the problem? And is either classifier an improvement over the room allocations made by physicians? These questions can be answered by examining visits to the emergency room by patients suspected of having acute ischemic heart disease. But how should one measure performance?

Classification error is the proportion of instances that are classified incorrectly. In the coronary care problem, this is the proportion of patients who are incorrectly assigned to the coronary care unit (when they do not have acute ischemic heart disease) or incorrectly assigned to a regular nursing bed (when they do have acute ischemic heart disease). Classification error has the advantage of summarizing performance with a single number but can be a misleading metric because it does not differentiate between the two different types of error.

Any binary classification problem has two possible types of error and two possible types of correct classifications. To discuss these generally, rather than specifically for the coronary care problem, we will use generic class names: *positive* and *negative*. In the coronary care problem, the positive class will denote the coronary care unit, and the negative class a regular nursing bed. The four possible outcomes of a classification, displayed in figure 2.3, are as follows.

A *hit* occurs if a positive instance is correctly classified as positive. This is a patient who has acute ischemic heart disease and is assigned to the coronary care unit. A hit is also known as a *true positive*.

A *miss* occurs if a positive instance is incorrectly classified as negative. In the coronary care problem, this is a patient who has acute ischemic heart disease but is assigned to a regular nursing bed. A miss is also known as a *false negative*.

A *false alarm* occurs if a negative instance is incorrectly classified as positive. This is a patient who does not have acute ischemic heart disease but is

		True class: Positive	True class: Negative
Predicted class	Positive	Hit	False alarm
	Negative	Miss	Correct rejection

Figure 2.3
Four possible outcomes in a binary classification problem.

assigned to the coronary care unit. A false alarm is also known as a *false positive.*

A *correct rejection* occurs if a negative instance is correctly classified as negative. This is a patient who does not have acute ischemic heart disease and is assigned to a regular nursing bed. A correct rejection is also known as a *true negative.*

In general, the two types of error differ in importance. For instance, it may be much more important to prevent a miss than to prevent a false alarm. In a laboratory experiment, the relative importance of misses and false alarms is set by the experimenter. In the wild, by contrast, it is usually impossible to quantify exactly—or even approximately—their importance. Ideally, both types of errors should be measured and reported. This is usually done by specifying the hit rate and the false alarm rate.

Hit rate is the number of hits divided by the total number of hits and misses. It answers the following question: if the true class is positive, what is the probability that the instance will be correctly classified as positive? For example, out of one hundred patients who have the disease, how many will be classified as having the disease? The ideal classifier has a hit rate of 100 percent, or 1. In medicine, the hit rate of a medical test is known as *sensitivity*.

False alarm rate is the number of false alarms divided by the total number of false alarms and correct rejections. It answers the following question: if the true class is negative, what is the probability that the instance will be incorrectly classified as positive? For example, out of one hundred patients who do not have the disease, how many will be classified as having the disease? The ideal classifier has a false alarm rate of 0. The complement of the false alarm rate is the correct rejection rate; the two rates add up to 1. In medicine, the correct rejection rate of a medical test is known as *specificity*.

To evaluate a classifier, or a medical test, one needs both the hit rate and the false alarm rate. Reporting only the hit rate is misleading. Unfortunately, such reports happen again and again, even on critical issues such as health care. In 2019 a press release from the University of Heidelberg reported that a new blood test had been developed for detecting breast cancer. The press release called the new test "a milestone in breast cancer diagnosis," and a front-page headline in *Bild Zeitung*, the most popular German tabloid, hailed it as a "world sensation." Both the press release and the tabloid reported that the test had a hit rate of 75 percent. Neither the press release nor the tabloid mentioned the false alarm rate.

One can easily avoid any misses and achieve a 100 percent hit rate by simply diagnosing every single woman with breast cancer. After scientists widely reported that a hit rate without the corresponding false alarm rate means nothing, the university researchers eventually revealed the false alarm rate of the test.[4] Across all groups tested, the average false alarm rate was 46 percent, meaning that roughly every other woman who does not have breast cancer would be diagnosed as having breast cancer by this test. In comparison, mammography screening has a hit rate of around 80 percent and a false alarm rate of around 5 to 10 percent, depending mainly on age.

To introduce a screening test with such a poor false alarm rate would be a public health disaster. Furthermore, after being screened by such a blood test, the unfortunate recipients of false alarms would have to live for up to five years with uncertainty before the result could be verified by mammography and other means. The test was eventually retracted.

One of the motivations for the press release was to market the blood test as quickly as possible. The apparently sensational discovery positively influenced the stock price of the pharmaceutical company involved, which led to a criminal investigation. The point of the investigation was not the potential harm to women but suspicion of price manipulation on the stock market.

To better understand the interplay between hit rates and false alarm rates, consider the left-hand panel of figure 2.4. The hit rate is shown on the vertical axis, and the false alarm rate on the horizontal axis. First, imagine a classifier that automatically classifies all instances as positive. This classifier has the ideal hit rate of 100 percent. But it also has the worst possible false alarm rate of 100 percent. Similarly, a classifier that automatically classifies

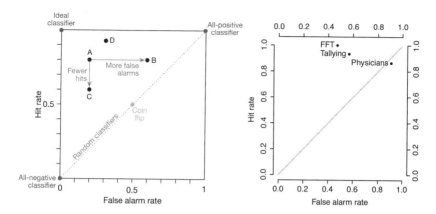

Figure 2.4
Left: Performance of various classifiers can be evaluated by comparing false alarm rates and hit rates. *Right*: Performance of Tallying for Coronary Care, Fast-and-Frugal Tree (FFT) for Coronary Care, and physicians on data collected by Lee Green and David Mehr.

all instances as negative has the ideal false alarm rate of 0 percent but also the worst possible hit rate of 0 percent. These two classifiers are depicted as the all-positive and the all-negative classifiers in the figure.

Next, imagine a classifier that flips a coin, assigning the instance to the positive class if the coin comes up heads or to the negative class if the coin comes up tails. This classifier has equal false alarm and hit rates of 50 percent. Other random classifiers are possible, for example, one that classifies the instance as positive if the coin comes up heads twice in a row, negative otherwise, resulting in equal false alarm and hit rates of 25 percent. Random classifiers of this type occupy the diagonal line (equal false alarm and hit rates) stretching from 0 percent to 100 percent. Below the diagonal are classifiers that perform worse than chance level. Above the diagonal are classifiers that perform better than chance level. The ideal classifier appears in the top left corner, with a 100 percent hit rate and 0 percent false alarm rate.

The figure also shows four hypothetical classifiers, A, B, C, and D. All are above the diagonal, indicating that they classify better than chance. Which one is the best classifier?

Classifier A is better than classifier C because it has a higher hit rate while having the same false alarm rate. Similarly, A is better than B because it has a lower false alarm rate while having the same hit rate. However, we cannot conclude whether A is better than D: although A has the lower false alarm rate, D has the higher hit rate. Whether A or D is the better classifier for the problem at hand depends on the relative importance of the two errors, misses and false alarms.

The right-hand panel of figure 2.4 shows the performance of the two fast-and-frugal classifiers in the coronary care problem on data collected by Lee Green and David Mehr at a Michigan hospital.[5] It also shows physicians' classification performance at the same hospital. Of the patients who had acute ischemic heart disease, physicians sent 86 percent correctly to the coronary care unit. Of the patients who did not have the disease, 91 percent were incorrectly sent to the coronary care unit. The performance of the physicians is slightly worse than chance, as depicted in the figure.

Why did the physicians send the vast majority of the incoming patients to the coronary care unit although only about a sixth of them (15 out of 89) actually had acute ischemic heart disease? This pattern can be explained by defensive decision making, similar to when magistrates make jail-or-bail decisions, as explained in chapter 1. Physicians are likely to be sued for a miss but not for a false alarm. Therefore the physicians in question protected themselves by sending almost everyone to the coronary care unit. As a consequence, the coronary care unit was overcrowded, quality of care was low, and costs were high. These circumstances motivated the search for better classifiers.

In contrast to the physicians' performance, that of both tallying and the fast-and-frugal tree are above the diagonal, indicating performance better than chance. Tallying has a hit rate of 93 percent and a false alarm rate of 57 percent. Compared with the physicians, both the hit rate and false alarm rate of tallying are better. The fast-and-frugal tree is superior to both physicians and tallying, with a hit rate of 100 percent and a false alarm rate of 47 percent.

These results demonstrate that fast-and-frugal classifiers can improve on allocations performed by physicians themselves. But we must exercise caution before reaching any conclusions, because the physicians who developed the fast-and-frugal classifiers may have based some of their design decisions on the same data on which the classifiers were evaluated. We describe this potential pitfall in the next section.

Before doing so, we first explain two concepts that are often confused with hit rates and false alarm rates. Assume a hospital that uses the Fast-and-Frugal Tree for Coronary Care, with a hit rate of 100 percent and a false alarm rate of 47 percent. A patient is rushed to this hospital and is assigned to the coronary care unit. What is the probability that the patient actually has acute ischemic heart disease? Is it 100 percent or 47 percent? Neither. This probability is called the *positive predictive value*. It requires a different division of the instances from the one used to calculate hit and false alarm rates.

Hit and false alarm rates divide the population into positive and negative instances, for example, people who have the disease and people who do not. The population can also be divided according to how they are classified: people who are classified as positive and people who are classified as negative, for example, patients who are placed into the coronary care unit and patients who are sent to a regular nursing bed. By using this division, we obtain two alternative performance metrics, positive predictive value and negative predictive value. These metrics are used frequently in medicine.

Positive predictive value is the number of hits divided by the total number of hits and false alarms. It answers the following question: if the instance is classified as positive, what is the probability that it is in fact positive? For example, out of one hundred patients who have been allocated to the coronary care unit, how many actually have acute ischemic heart disease? The ideal classifier has a positive predictive value of 100 percent.

Negative predictive value is the number of correct rejections divided by the total number of correct rejections and misses. It answers the following question: if the instance is classified as negative, what is the probability that it is in fact negative? For example, out of one hundred patients who have been sent to a regular nursing bed, how many do not actually have acute ischemic heart disease? The ideal classifier has a negative predictive value of 100 percent.

Positive predictive value (PPV) and negative predictive value (NPV) can be computed from the number of hits, misses, false alarms, and correct rejections. They can also be computed from the hit rate and false alarm rate if a third quantity is known: base rate. The *base rate* is the proportion of positive instances in a population, also known as *prevalence*. In the coronary care problem, the base rate is the proportion of patients with ischemic heart disease among those who arrive at the hospital emergency room. For completeness, we present here how PPV and NPV can be computed from sensitivity, specificity, and prevalence using Bayes' rule.

$$PPV= \frac{prevalence \times sensitivity}{prevalence \times sensitivity + (1-prevalence)(1-specificity)}$$

$$NPV= \frac{(1-prevalence) \times specificity}{(1-prevalence) \times specificity + prevalence \times (1-sensitivity)}$$

In Bayesian statistics, positive predictive value and negative predictive value are called the *posterior* probabilities, while the base rate corresponds to the *prior* probability of the positive class.

2.5 Understanding Classifier Performance

The concepts of hit rate, false alarm rate, positive predictive value, and negative predictive value are routinely confused in medicine, in law, and elsewhere. For example, it is easy to confuse the probability that a woman will get a positive mammogram result if she has breast cancer with the probability that a woman has breast cancer if she gets a positive mammogram result. The first one is the hit rate, the second the positive predictive value. In mammography screening for breast cancer, the hit rate is about 80 percent, and the positive predictive value around 10 percent. Exact values are difficult to compute in the wild.

To illustrate the confusion, try to answer the following four questions from the Quick Risk Test.[6]

1. Which of the following correctly defines sensitivity?

    a. The proportion of people with a positive test result among those who are sick

    b. The proportion of people with a negative test result among those who are sick

    c. The proportion of people with a positive test result among those who are healthy

    d. The proportion of people with a negative test result among those who are healthy

2. Which of the following correctly defines specificity?

   a. The proportion of people with a positive test result among those who are sick

   b. The proportion of people with a negative test result among those who are sick

   c. The proportion of people with a positive test result among those who are healthy

   d. The proportion of people with a negative test result among those who are healthy

3. Which test characteristic quantifies the probability that a person with a positive test result actually has the disease?

   a. Positive predictive value

   b. Negative predictive value

   c. Specificity

   d. Sensitivity

4. Which test characteristic quantifies the probability that a person with a negative test result does not have the disease?

   a. Positive predictive value

   b. Negative predictive value

   c. Specificity

   d. Sensitivity

To understand these concepts is essential in medicine.[7] Otherwise no test result can be evaluated properly. Nevertheless, a study at the Charité University of Medicine in Berlin, one of the leading medical hospitals in Europe, revealed that a considerable proportion of students in their final year of study could not answer these four questions correctly. A similar result was found for professors at another medical school, senior physicians, and lecturers in medicine, as shown in figure 2.5. The participants in the study were 169 final-year medical students and 16 professors of medicine and other senior educators. Because the questions have four alternatives, one can expect 25 percent accuracy by blind chance. Only about 80 percent of students and professors could identify the correct definition of sensitivity. Only about 60 to 65 percent of students and professors were

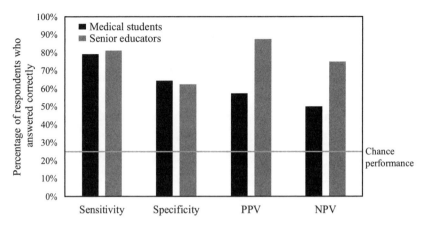

Figure 2.5

Limited knowledge of key concepts among medical students and senior educators. The graph shows the percentage of correct answers by final-year medical students and by senior educators (professors, senior physicians, and university lecturers) to each of the four questions listed in the text. PPV = positive predictive value; NPV = negative predictive value. The horizontal line indicates chance performance (25 percent). The questions are part of the Quick Risk Test in Jenny, Keller, and Gigerenzer, "Assessing Minimal Medical Statistical Literacy Using the Quick Risk Test: A Prospective Observational Study in Germany," *British Medical Journal Open* 8, no. 8 (2018): e020847.

able to identify specificity. Fewer than 60 percent of the students knew what positive predictive value is; only about 55 percent knew what negative predictive value is. Medical students and teachers who do not understand these concepts are not able to evaluate the outcome of medical tests such as screening tests for HIV, COVID-19, and cancer.

2.6   Fitting, Predicting Out of Sample, and Predicting Out of Population

Building a classifier means determining its parameters. For a linear classifier such as logistic regression, the parameters are the weights of the cues and the additive constant. For tallying, the parameters are the target, threshold, and reasons. For a fast-and-frugal tree, the parameters are the reasons, their exits, and their order.

In practice, a useful method for determining the parameters of a classifier is to estimate them from instances for which the correct class is known.

An example is a patient who arrives at the emergency room and is later diagnosed with acute ischemic heart disease. Such instances are called *training instances*. The set of training instances is called a *training set*.

When parameters are estimated from examples, an important principle is that the performance of the classifier should not be evaluated on the basis of instances that were used in estimating the parameters.

A widespread but questionable practice is fitting. *Fitting* refers to cases in which the same data are used to estimate both the classifier parameters and the classifier performance. The Texas sharpshooter story illustrates how one can be misled by impressive results obtained via data fitting. The left-hand panel in figure 2.6 shows the performance of our sharpshooter after shooting at the side of a barn with a revolver from one hundred meters away. Performance appears to be quite good. What is not said, however, is that the sharpshooter painted the bull's-eye *after* shooting, to fit the bullet holes as well as possible. The panel on the right-hand side of the figure shows the bullet holes before the bull's-eye was painted.

The Texas sharpshooter shoots first and then fits the bull's-eye to the bullet holes. With one free parameter, we can move the bull's-eye from left to right; with two parameters, we can adjust it across the entire surface of the barn wall. Shooting first before drawing the target corresponds to data fitting. "With four parameters, I can fit an elephant," John von Neumann has said, "and with five I can make him wiggle his trunk."[8]

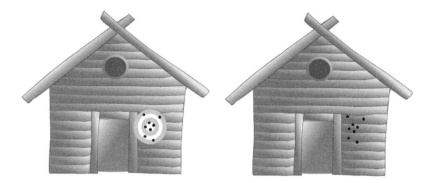

Figure 2.6
Texas sharpshooter. The impressive accuracy of the sharpshooter (*left*) is obtained by shooting at the barn first (*right*) and afterward painting the bull's-eye and the target rings around the bullet holes.

Free parameters of a classification rule make it possible to adjust the rule so that the classification rule fits the data as closely as possible. The more flexible the classification rule is, the more likely it will adjust to the idiosyncrasies of a given training set. This is known as *overfitting*. A classification rule that overfits to the training data will not perform as well when applied to new instances.

In the Texas sharpshooter story, the problem is that the same data (bullet holes in the barn wall) were used both to construct a "model" (where the shooter was aiming) and to test the "model" (the accuracy of the shots). It is easy to see that, measured in this way, the accuracy of the shots does not truly reflect the accuracy of the sharpshooter. So it is with data fitting. When we use the same data set both to determine the parameters of the classification rule and to measure the performance of the classification rule, we do not obtain a true measure of performance. Instead we need to measure performance on a different data set. This is called *prediction* as opposed to fitting.

We distinguish between two types of prediction. Out-of-sample prediction occurs when parameters are estimated on a randomly drawn subset of the population (a random sample) and the classifier will be used on a different random sample from the same population. For example, taking data collected in a hospital over a period of four weeks, one could use half of the instances (selected randomly from the data set) to estimate the parameters of the classification rule, and the other half to estimate the performance of the classification rule.

Out-of-population prediction occurs when the population on which the classifier will be used is different from the population on which the classifier was developed. For example, the Keys to the White House were developed using past presidential elections in the United States with the intention to predict the outcome of future elections. This is out-of-population prediction because the population of American voters changes from election to election. Similarly, in health care, classification rules are developed in one patient population (e.g., in Boston) and applied in different ones (e.g., in Michigan). In the wild, out-of-population prediction is the most relevant because the future can differ from the past in unpredictable ways.

The assumption of stable hit rates, stable false alarm rates, and the like requires a stable world. In the wild, stability is not possible. This makes developing classifiers in the wild challenging.

Nevertheless, classification in the wild is indispensable. Almost every real-world application of classification takes place there. Looking at out-of-sample performance criteria such as hit rates can serve as a guideline without any guarantees that we will obtain the same performance in the future. It also reminds us not to overfit by trying to fine-tune past samples.

3 Building Fast-and-Frugal Classifiers

Make things as simple as possible, but not simpler.
—attributed to Albert Einstein

Building a fast-and-frugal classifier starts by pinpointing various pieces of information (cues) that can be useful in identifying the class of an instance. In HIV screening, useful cues include outcomes of blood tests, such as the ELISA and Western blot; in allocating emergency treatment at a disaster site, cues include whether the victim can breathe or walk. An important source of insight in identifying cues is domain expertise. For example, the Keys to the White House were developed based on analysis of earlier presidential elections in the United States by a professor of history. Similarly, START (Simple Triage and Rapid Treatment) embodies the extensive practical experience of emergency personnel at disaster sites.

How should we combine the various pieces of information? Here fast-and-frugal classification provides strong guidelines: cues are either ordered or tallied. Many design choices remain, however. For example, in HIV screening, should we perform an ELISA test before or after a Western blot test? In the Keys to the White House, should the fact that the incumbent party candidate is the sitting president count in favor of or against the challenger? How many keys suffice to predict a victory for the challenger: five, six, seven, or more?

To answer such questions, domain expertise once again proves useful. Expertise is the art in building a classifier. A second source of insight is statistical information. For instance, data from large samples of people are available on the hit and false alarm rates of existing HIV diagnostic tests.

In spite of its limitations, as discussed in chapter 1, researchers—sometimes even people with little domain expertise—can use such statistical information fruitfully to build a fast-and-frugal classifier. How to use statistical information is the science of building fast-and-frugal classifiers. It is the subject of the present chapter. Later on, in chapter 6, we discuss the art of using domain knowledge in what we call the practitioner method of building fast-and-frugal classifiers, and how the art can be combined with the science.

To simplify the exposition, we ignore many sources of uncertainty that are characteristic of the wild, such as limited reliability and availability of data. We focus instead on the following question: how can data, if available and accurate, guide the development of a fast-and-frugal classifier? To illustrate various methods, we continue to use the coronary care problem described in chapter 2.

3.1 Looking at Each Cue in Isolation

We begin with a very simple classifier, one that uses a single piece of information. Consider one of the cues in the coronary care problem, chest pain, and assume that it is the only available cue. What is the best way to classify using this cue?

Two options are available, as shown in figure 3.1. Classifier A allocates the patient to the coronary care unit if chest pain is present, otherwise to a regular nursing bed. Classifier B does the opposite. Which one is the better classifier? Is having chest pain a reason for allocating the patient to the coronary care unit or to a regular nursing bed?

Intuitively, the reason to send the patient to the coronary care unit is the presence of chest pain, not its absence. In this particular case, intuition can be checked by data. Figure 3.1 shows the four outcomes from each classifier in the data set: hits, false alarms, misses, and correct rejections. These are shown separately at each exit from the tree. Notice that assigning a patient to a regular nursing bed can lead to only two possible outcomes: a miss or a correct rejection. Similarly, assigning a patient to the coronary care unit can lead to only a hit or a false alarm. The figure also shows the performance of the two classifiers by plotting hit rate against the false alarm rate. Recall that the diagonal line on the plot shows random classification.

The data support our intuition: classifier A performs better than random, and classifier B worse than random, in our data set. But classifier A is not

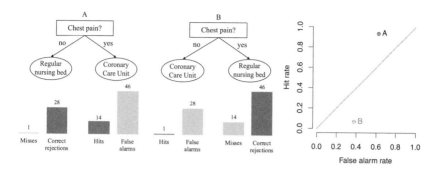

Figure 3.1

In the coronary care problem, when using only chest pain to distinguish between the classes, two classifiers are possible. The patient is allocated to the coronary care unit if chest pain is present (classifier A) or absent (classifier B). Classifier A is the intuitive choice. Indeed, in our data set, classifier A performs better than random, and classifier B performs worse than random.

particularly good, either. While its hit rate is high, its false alarm rate is also extremely high. Many patients with chest pain do not have acute ischemic heart disease.

Classifier A is said to use the cue in the *positive direction* because the higher cue value (present, 1) is associated with the class that has the higher numerical value (coronary care unit, 1), as shown in table 2.1. Analogously, classifier B is said to use the cue in the *negative direction*. Transparency is usually improved by coding cues and classes so that the higher cue value is associated with the class that has the higher numerical value. This is what we have done. For chest pain, which is a known symptom of heart attack, the cue value "present" was given the same high value as the class "coronary care unit," and the cue value "absent" was given the same low value as the class "regular nursing bed."

Intuition is a useful guide, but it is not always accurate. Consider another cue identified by physicians as diagnostic of acute ischemic heart disease, ST barring. This cue shows whether the electrocardiogram shows an abnormally straightened or barred ST segment. The intuitive choice is to allocate the patient to the coronary care unit if ST barring is present, otherwise to a regular nursing bed. But this classifier performs worse than chance, as seen in figure 3.2, which shows the hit and false alarm rates of all seven cues in both the positive and the negative direction. ST barring, when used in

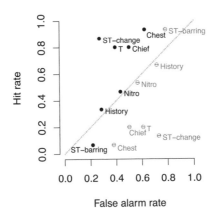

Figure 3.2
Hit rates and false alarm rates for all seven cues in the coronary care problem, when each cue is used in isolation. The figure shows performance when the cue is used in both the positive direction (filled circles) and the negative direction (open circles with a negative sign drawn in the middle).

the positive direction, has a false alarm rate of 0.22 and a hit rate of 0.07. This counterintuitive result could be an artifact of our data set being too small to obtain a reliable estimate of the effect of this cue. Alternatively, ST barring, although an abnormality, may not predict acute ischemic heart disease among our patient population.

Which Cue Is Best on Its Own?

Consider the seven cues identified by physicians in the coronary care problem (table 2.1). If we were limited to using only one of these cues, how should we pick?

The visual display of hit rates and false alarm rates in figure 3.2 provides an informative guide. The data suggest that ST change and chest pain *dominate* all other cues, meaning that all other cues show a lower hit rate and a higher false alarm rate than one or both of these cues. But which cue is better: ST change or chest pain? The answer depends on the relative importance of the two possible errors. Chest pain causes a large increase in false alarm rate compared with ST change while increasing hit rate by a relatively small amount.

Tallying or Fast-and-Frugal Tree?

Figure 3.2 gives us a hint about whether tallying or a fast-and-frugal tree will lead to better classifications. Some of the cues show much better performance on their own than others, as measured by their hit rates and false alarm rates. For instance, nitroglycerin and history perform very close to chance level, whereas ST change and chest pain perform much better. These data support a priority ordering among the cues, suggesting that a fast-and-frugal tree may be the better approach.

We now consider different ways of combining the cues to arrive at an effective classifier. We begin with tallying, which is the simpler model, requiring fewer parameters.

3.2   Building Tallying Rules

Building a tallying rule starts with choosing the target class. This choice gives us flexibility, because equivalent tallying rules can be written for different target classes. For instance, the Keys to the White House can be written so that the predicted winner of the election remains the same, but the keys count toward a win for the incumbent rather than the challenger. Nonetheless, the designated target class can make a difference in how easily the decision rule is understood and communicated. Generally, the target class is the one observed less frequently, for example, a positive HIV diagnosis. The classification rule then explains the unusual classification rather than the typical one.

The second step is to identify the reasons. Once we identify the cues, all that remains is to decide on cue directions. One simple but surprisingly effective approach is to decide on each cue direction independently of the others. In some cases, domain knowledge is enough. For example, a positive ELISA test supports an HIV diagnosis. In other cases, examining hit and false alarm rates is informative (see fig. 3.2).

Finally, we need to choose a threshold. The threshold determines how easily the classifier assigns instances to the target class. Figure 3.3 shows the effect of the threshold on Tallying for Coronary Care. The two bar charts show the exact number of reasons that are satisfied in the two patient groups: those who have acute ischemic heart disease (top panel) and those who do not (bottom panel). For instance, among the patients who have the disease, for no patient are zero, one, or two reasons satisfied, whereas for three patients, six reasons are satisfied.

The threshold divides each plot into two regions. Patients allocated to a regular nursing bed are on the left-hand side of the threshold, and those allocated to the coronary care unit are on the right-hand side of the threshold. Accordingly, the figure shows each of the four possible outcomes of classification: misses (top left), hits (top right), correct rejections (bottom left), and false alarms (bottom right). As the threshold increases, the classifier sends fewer and fewer people to the coronary care unit. As the threshold decreases, the classifier sends more and more people to the coronary care unit.

Notice that increasing the threshold has two simultaneous effects: reducing the number of false alarms but also the hits. Similarly, decreasing the threshold increases the number of hits but also the false alarms. We can see the effect of the threshold more clearly in the right-hand panel of figure 3.3, which shows hit and false alarm rates for various values of the threshold. This graphical plot is known as *the receiver operating characteristic* (ROC) curve. For completeness, we include thresholds of zero and eight here. With a threshold of zero, the classifier sends all patients to the coronary care unit without discrimination. With a threshold of eight, the classifier sends none of the patients to the coronary care unit, again without discrimination (because there are only seven reasons).

Which threshold is the best? The figure shows that thresholds from three to seven dominate the rest. Choosing among these threshold values depends on the relative importance of misses and false alarms. Tallying for Coronary Care uses a threshold of three, which reflects a strong preference for avoiding misses relative to false alarms.

Now we are ready to present a full algorithm for building a tallying classifier. We address the simple case of binary classification with binary cues with an algorithm we call Basic Tallying.

Basic Tallying: This is an algorithm that learns the parameters of a tallying classifier for binary classification with binary cues. Its building blocks are as follows:

1. Set the target to the class that is observed less frequently.
2. Create one reason for each available cue by setting cue direction to the direction that performs better than chance in the training set. This can

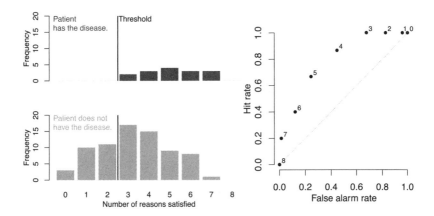

Figure 3.3
The impact of the threshold on the performance of Tallying for Coronary Care. See the text for details.

be evaluated by comparing hit and false alarm rates when the cue is used in the positive and the negative direction (see fig. 3.2). Consider dropping some of the cues, for example, if the performance of a cue is close to chance level.

3. Plot the ROC curve (see fig. 3.3), which shows the hit rate and the false alarm rate produced by each value of the threshold. Set the threshold to the value that provides the most suitable trade-off between misses and false alarms, given their relative importance. In the wild, judging this relative importance may be difficult and is part of the art of classification.

4. Examine the resulting tallying rule. Can the transparency of the rule be improved by changing the target class? Or by rephrasing one or more of the reasons? For example, asking whether the candidate is charismatic may yield a classification rule that is easier to understand and explain than asking whether the candidate lacks charisma.

We now apply this algorithm to the coronary care problem. Of the eighty-nine patients for whom we have data, fifteen were eventually diagnosed with the disease and therefore should have been allocated to the coronary care unit.[1] The remaining seventy-four patients did not have the disease and therefore should have been allocated to a regular nursing bed.

The algorithm sets the target to coronary care unit because this is the class observed less frequently. Next, looking at figure 3.2, we decide to discard the three cues history, nitroglycerin, and ST barring because their performance is too close to chance. From the figure, we observe that the remaining four cues perform better than chance when used in the positive direction. We therefore set cue directions to positive. The final parameter to be set is the threshold. To do this, we plot the ROC curve, as shown in figure 3.4. A threshold of two or three appears to be the most suitable. We can describe the trade-off between these two thresholds as follows: among 100 patients with acute ischemic heart disease and 100 patients without, increasing the threshold from 2 to 3 would decrease hits by 7 and false alarms by 26. Note that these numbers show performance in the training set; actual performance in the wild may differ.

3.3   Working with Numerical Cues

The financial crisis of 2007–2008 started with problems in the subprime mortgage market in the United States and quickly developed into an international banking crisis. Many global banks failed and had to be bailed out. Could analysts have predicted the failing banks in advance? We discuss

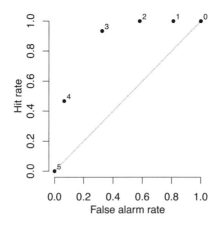

Figure 3.4
The classifier produced by the Basic Tallying algorithm. The choice of the threshold is informed by the ROC curve, as described in the text.

this problem in detail in chapter 6. Here we examine a numerical cue, the leverage ratio, that is useful for predicting bank failure.

The *leverage ratio* is defined as the ratio of a bank's Tier 1 capital, including capital from common stock and disclosed reserves, to its total assets. It measures how much of a bank's capital derives from debt, and is useful in assessing whether a bank can meet its financial obligations. For instance, someone who buys an apartment for $100,000 but has only $10,000 and takes a mortgage for the remaining $90,000 has a leverage ratio of 10,000 / 100,000 = 10 percent. Higher values of the leverage ratio are safer.

The left-hand panel of figure 3.5 shows the distribution of leverage ratios for 110 global banks that had more than US$100 billion in assets at the end of 2006.[2] The leverage ratios ranged from 1.41 percent to 9.28 percent. Of the 110 banks, 39 failed within the next two years. These banks are described as "failing," and the rest are described as "healthy." The figure shows that healthy banks tend to have higher leverage ratios.

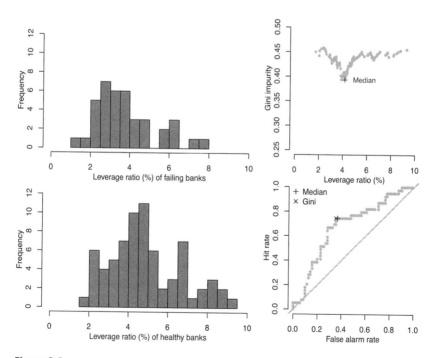

Figure 3.5

Leverage ratio of 110 global banks at the end of 2006. This numerical cue can be converted into a binary one by using the median or Gini impurity.

How can we use a numerical cue such as the leverage ratio in tallying? A simple and effective approach is to convert the numerical cue into a binary cue that shows whether the cue value is below or above a given threshold. The only parameter in this approach is the cue threshold. This threshold can be set to the median cue value in the training set. For example, leverage ratio can be converted to a binary cue that shows whether a bank's leverage ratio is below or above the median leverage ratio of the banks in the training set.

Is there a better approach? Let us consider what an ideal threshold would look like. A threshold splits the instances into two groups that may be treated differently by the classifier. For example, the classifier can assign the banks whose leverage ratio is below the threshold to the failing class and the instances above the threshold to the healthy class. If a threshold is ideal, all failing banks will be below the threshold, and all healthy banks will be above the threshold. The resulting binary cue would then classify all banks in the training set with perfect accuracy. In practice, we cannot expect such perfect separation of the classes. But we can set the threshold to the value that most closely approaches this ideal.

What we are aiming for in each group of banks, below and above the threshold, is *purity*. If banks in one group are all healthy, or all failing, then this group has perfect purity. On the other hand, if in one group half of the banks are healthy and the other half are failing, then this group has the lowest possible purity. We need a measure of purity that reflects these observations. One such measure is the *Gini impurity*.

The Gini impurity is the probability of making a wrong classification if a random member of the group is classified according to the frequency distribution in the group. It equals $2p(1 - p)$, where p is the proportion of instances in the group that belong to one class, such as the class of failing banks (then $1 - p$ is the proportion of instances that belong to the other class). For example, if the group has one failing bank and three healthy banks, then with probability ¼ an instance selected randomly will be a failing bank. Following the frequency distribution in the group, this bank will be classified as failing with probability ¼ and as healthy with probability ¾. Thus a failing bank will be classified incorrectly with probability ¾. Conversely, with probability ¾, the instance selected will be a healthy bank, and with probability ¼, it will be classified incorrectly. Considering both classifications, the probability of an incorrect classification is ¼ × ¾ + ¾ × ¼ = 2 × ¼ × ¾ = 0.375. This is the Gini impurity of the group of four banks.

Each threshold divides the banks into two groups, those below the threshold and those above the threshold. The Gini impurity of this whole *grouping* is the weighted average of the Gini impurities of the two groups, where the weights are the proportions of instances in each group. To maximize purity, we choose a threshold that minimizes the Gini impurity of the grouping produced by the threshold.

The top right-hand panel in figure 3.5 shows how the Gini impurity varies with the threshold. Threshold values slightly below four achieve the best separation of the classes, as measured by Gini impurity. This panel also shows the median leverage ratio in the data set. It happens to be very close to the threshold that minimizes Gini impurity. In the bottom right-hand panel are the hit and false alarm rates when the resulting binary cue is used as a classifier by itself. This panel shows the threshold that minimizes Gini impurity, along with the threshold that equals the median leverage ratio.

Other ways exist to choose the threshold, for example, by using the ROC curve itself. An alternative to the Gini impurity is Shannon entropy, defined as $-p \log_2 p - (1 - p) \log_2(1 - p)$, where p is the proportion of instances belonging to one class, as defined earlier.

3.4 Building Fast-and-Frugal Trees

We now turn to the question of how to build fast-and-frugal trees. We assume that there are only two classes, and all cues are binary. Any numerical cues can be converted to binary ones, as discussed in the previous section. If the relative cost of a miss compared with that of a false alarm is known, then this information can be used.

A Basic Method for Building Fast-and-Frugal Trees

A fast-and-frugal tree creates a priority ordering among the cues. What should this ordering be? An ideal binary cue splits instances into two branches such that the class distribution is pure in each branch. This ideal is rarely observed in practice, but once again we can use Gini impurity to approximately measure how closely the various cues approach this ideal. The Basic Fast-and-Frugal Tree algorithm orders the cues in increasing order of their Gini impurity, placing the cue with the lowest Gini impurity at the root of the tree. It determines cue directions in the same way that Basic Tallying does. Specifically, it uses each cue in the direction that performs better than chance in the training set, as measured by the hit rate and the false alarm rate when the cue is used as a classifier on its own (see fig. 3.2). The only part of the tree we are now missing is the *exit structure*, in other words, the locations of the exits in the tree.

Before describing how to determine the exit structure, we first note that a fast-and-frugal tree is a lexicographic classifier. The word *lexicographic* means "like a dictionary." A lexicographic classifier orders the instances just as a dictionary orders words. When deciding which of two words is defined first in a dictionary, we compare words letter by letter, from left to right, until we encounter a letter on which the two words differ. For example, the words *fast* and *frugal* are identical in their first letter but differ in their second. *Fast* precedes *frugal* because the letter *a* precedes the letter *r* in the English alphabet. All remaining letters of the two words are irrelevant.

The cue profile of an instance is analogous to a word. Consider the three cues in the Fast-and-Frugal Tree for Coronary Care in the order they are used: ST change, chief complaint, and any other symptom. Cue directions are all positive. Each cue will be represented by its numerical value, 0 (absent) or 1 (present). With three binary cues, we have eight possible cue profiles. For example, a patient with all three cues present is represented by cue profile 111, a patient with all three cues absent by 000, and a patient with ST change absent, chief complaint present, and any other symptom absent by 010.

Given the cue order and directions, a lexicographic classifier orders the eight cue profiles as follows, from the smallest to the largest: 000, 001, 010, 011, 100, 101, 110, 111. Consider the full tree with the same cue order and directions, as shown in figure 3.6. Notice that the eight exits of the tree at the bottom level each map to exactly one of these eight cue profiles. The cue profiles are arranged from left to right in their lexicographic order. A full tree is flexible; it can assign any cue profile to any class. A fast-and-frugal tree, however, is constrained: if it assigns a cue profile to the larger class (1, coronary care unit), then it must also assign all larger cue profiles to the same class. Similarly, if a fast-and-frugal tree assigns a cue profile to the smaller class (0, regular nursing bed), then it must also assign all smaller cue profiles to the same class.

One of the cue profiles is special. This is the largest cue profile for which the predicted class is the smaller class (regular nursing bed). It is called the *splitting profile*.[3] The splitting profile of the Fast-and-Frugal Tree for

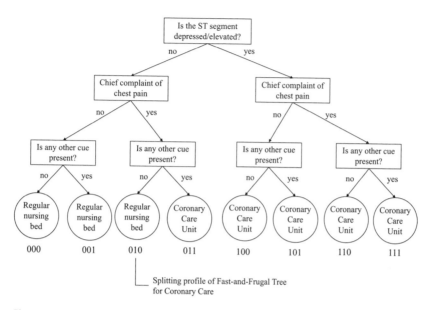

Figure 3.6
The full tree with cue order and directions identical to those of the Fast-and-Frugal Tree for Coronary Care (fig. 2.2), along with its splitting profile.

Coronary Care is 010, as indicated in figure 3.6, because it assigns patients with the cue profile 010 or lower to the regular nursing bed and patients with a cue profile larger than 010 to the coronary care unit. The splitting profile completely determines the exit structure of the fast-and-frugal tree. Figure 3.7 shows the fast-and-frugal trees defined by all possible splitting profiles. Note that some of these trees do not use all three cues.

We now return to the question of how to set the exit structure given that we have already determined cue order and cue directions. Each splitting profile specifies an exit structure. To select one of these fast-and-frugal trees, we compute the hit rate and false alarm rate of each tree. This forms an ROC curve. As in Basic Tallying, we examine the ROC curve to gain an insight into the trade-off between hits and false alarms and pick the tree best suited to the problem at hand. Figure 3.8 shows the corresponding ROC curve when cue order and cue directions are set to those of the Fast-and-Frugal Tree for Coronary Care. The trees are labeled using their splitting profiles. Notice that as the splitting profile increases lexicographically,

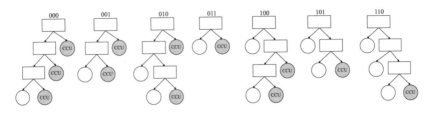

Figure 3.7
Fast-and-frugal trees corresponding to all possible splitting profiles. Exit leaves for coronary care unit are the gray circles labeled "CCU," and for regular nursing bed the empty circles. Where possible, the trees are simplified in structure. For example, if a question leads to two exits predicting the same class, the question and its two exits can be replaced by a single exit for the same class (the classifications of the tree remain the same). This is why some of the trees use fewer questions than others. The two extreme classifiers (and their splitting profiles), which classify all instances in the same way, are not shown in the figure.

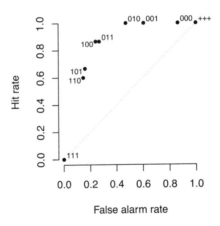

Figure 3.8
Hit rate and false alarm rate of fast-and-frugal trees with various splitting profiles when cue order and directions are those used by the Fast-and-Frugal Tree for Coronary Care. The all-negative classifier corresponds to splitting profile 111. The all-positive classifier is denoted by +++.

the fast-and-frugal tree less easily allocates patients to the coronary care unit, and both the hit rate and the false alarm rate progressively drop. We discuss the relationship between performance and the exit structure further in section 3.7.

This method requires computing the ROC curve with all possible exit structures, given cue order and cue directions. With k cues, there are $2^k + 1$ exit structures, a number that grows quickly with k. We therefore recommend limiting the depth of the tree.

Basic Fast-and-Frugal Tree: This is an algorithm that learns the parameters of a fast-and-frugal tree for binary classification with binary cues. Input parameter: d (maximum tree depth, with default value 3). Its building blocks are as follows:

1. Order cues in increasing order of their Gini impurity, discarding any cues other than those that have the d lowest Gini impurities.

2. Set direction of each cue (positive or negative) to the value that yields better-than-chance performance in the training set, as measured by hit rate and false alarm rate (see fig. 3.2).

3. Plot the ROC curve (see fig. 3.6), which shows the hit rate and the false alarm rate produced by the various exit structures. Choose the exit structure that provides the most suitable trade-off between hits and false alarms, given their relative importance for the problem at hand. In the wild, judging this relative importance may be difficult and is part of the art of classification.

4. Examine the resulting classification rule. Can the transparency of the rule be improved by rephrasing one or more of the reasons? For example, asking whether the patient has a history of heart attack may yield a classification rule that is easier to understand and explain than asking whether the patient lacks a history of heart attack.

Building Fast-and-Frugal Trees One Reason at a Time

We next describe a different method for building a fast-and-frugal tree that uses one reason at a time. To add the next reason, the algorithm takes into account the existing parts of the tree.

This algorithm starts by determining the first reason, including the cue to be used, its direction, and the exit. As in the Basic Fast-and-Frugal Tree algorithm, the cue is the one that yields the lowest Gini impurity. The direction is the one that performs better than chance, which we can easily see by plotting hit rate against false alarm rate (as in fig. 3.2). Cue direction determines the class prediction of each branch. One of these branches will be an exit from the tree, and the other branch—unless this is the last level of the tree—will split on a different cue. We now know the class prediction of each branch but do not yet know which branch will be the exit. To make that final decision for this level, we examine the Gini impurity of each branch; the exit is the branch with the lower Gini impurity.

The next step is to check whether any of the following termination conditions are reached: (1) all cues have been used; (2) all training instances have been classified in the existing levels of the tree; and (3) the tree has reached the maximum allowed depth set by the developer. If any of these conditions hold, then the remaining branch from the level is also made an exit, with the corresponding class prediction. Otherwise the process is repeated to identify the second level of the tree.

The next levels of the tree are built following the same process, with two differences. First, the cues that have been used in earlier levels are no longer considered. Second, the training instances are processed through the existing levels of the tree; those that exit the tree with a classification are set aside and not used any further. This means that the Gini impurity of the remaining cues is computed using only the training instances that remain in the tree.

How can one account for different user preferences in the relative importance of misses and false alarms? If a single miss and a single false alarm are equally undesirable, then there is nothing further to do. Otherwise the training set can be transformed so that it reflects our preference. We give two examples.

First, consider the case where a single miss and four false alarms are equally undesirable. In this case, the training set can be augmented by replicating each training instance in the positive class so that it appears four times. Second, consider another case where the miss rate and false alarm rate are equally important. In this case, the performance metric is the balanced accuracy, which equals the mean of hit rate and correct rejection rate. Let n_1 be the number of training instances in the majority class (the class with the larger number of training instances), and n_2 the number of training instances in the minority class. In this case, each training instance in the minority class is replicated so that it appears n_1/n_2 times. These adjustments to the training instances naturally reflect our preferences.

This method of building fast-and-frugal trees is called *greedy* because each level of the tree is determined by looking ahead only one level.

Greedy Fast-and-Frugal Tree: This is an algorithm that learns the parameters of a fast-and-frugal tree for binary classification with binary cues. Input parameter: maximum tree depth d. Its building blocks are as follows:

1. Determine the next reason of the tree: The cue is the one that yields the lowest Gini impurity. Its direction is the one that performs better than chance, which we can easily see by plotting hit rate against false alarm rate (as in fig. 3.2). The branch with the lower Gini impurity is the exit.

2. Check whether any of the following termination conditions are satisfied: (1) All cues have been used; (2) all training instances have been classified in the existing levels of the tree; and (3) the tree has reached the maximum allowed depth d. If any of these conditions hold, then create a second exit at the present level, completing the tree. Otherwise discard the training instances that are already classified and return to step 1 to identify the next reason of the tree.

3. Examine the resulting classification rule. Can the transparency of the rule be improved by rephrasing one or more of the reasons? For example, asking whether the patient has a history of heart attack may yield a classification rule that is easier to understand and explain than asking whether the patient lacks a history of heart attack.

3.5 Other Approaches and Online Resources

We can use other approaches to build fast-and-frugal trees.[4] Instead of using the hit rate (sensitivity) and false alarm rate (1–specificity) of cues, some approaches make design decisions based on the cues' positive and negative predictive values.

Another approach enumerates the space of all possible fast-and-frugal trees and picks the tree that achieves the best performance in the training set. For this approach to be tractable, the total number of cues needs to be limited to a small number. This method is called *Best Fit*. It can be applied to tallying, as well. We show applications of Best Fit in chapters 4 and 6.

We provide several algorithms for building fast-and-frugal classifiers in an R package called *ffcr* (fast-and-frugal classification in R). The package includes the coronary care problem and other data sets used in this book. Other resources include the R package FFTrees and the Adaptive Toolbox website of the Max Planck Institute for Human Development in Berlin.[5]

3.6   Examples

We now apply these fast-and-frugal classifiers in the following six environments. Each environment consists of instances that are described by their class and cue values.

Broadway: Determine whether a Broadway show will survive more than six months based on type (musical, musical revue, or play), number of viewers in the first week, number of Tony Award nominations received, number of Tony Awards won, rating of the show by the *New York Times*, rating of the show by the *Daily News*, and whether the show is a revival. The environment contains 95 shows that opened on Broadway between 1996 and 1999. Of these, 27 shows survived more than six months; 68 shows did not.[6]

Frog: Determine whether the southern corroboree frog is present or absent in 212 sites in the Snowy Mountains range in New South Wales. Available cues are altitude, distance to nearest extant population, number of potential breeding pools, number of potential breeding sites within a radius of two kilometers, average rainfall in spring, minimum temperature in spring, maximum temperature in spring, northing, and easting. The species was present in 79 sites, absent in 133 sites.[7]

SMS: Determine whether or not an SMS is spam. Available cues are frequencies of 1,418 words such as *get*, *cheap*, and *much*. The environment contains 5,574 SMS, of which 747 are spam and 4,827 are not.[8]

Digits: Determine whether an image shows the digit 4 or 9. Available cues are numeric variables, each representing the grayscale values of 1 of the $28 \times 28 = 784$ pixels of an image. The environment contains 13,782 grayscale images. Of these, 6,824 images showed the digit 4, and 6,958 images showed digit 9. The original data set contains images of all digits from 0 to 9. We chose the images of the rather similar-looking digits 4 and 9 to reduce the data to a binary classification problem.[9]

Voice: Determine whether a voice sample comes from a female or a male given twenty acoustic properties of the voice sample, such as the mean frequency, median frequency, spectral flatness, and minimum of dominant frequency measures across the acoustic signal. The environment contains 3,168 preprocessed voice samples, of which 1,584 come from a female.[10]

Star: Determine whether or not a space observation is of a galaxy. Available cues are astronomical coordinates (right ascension, declination), redshift, and five measurements of the response of a 5 bands telescope. The environment contains 10,000 observations of space. Of these, 4,998 are of a galaxy, and 5,002 are not (being either of a star or of a quasar).[11]

In each environment, we tested Basic Tallying, Basic Fast-and-Frugal Tree, and Greedy Fast-and-Frugal Tree. The fast-and-frugal classifiers were limited to using no more than six cues. As a baseline, we included results from logistic regression. One version of logistic regression is directly comparable to the fast-and-frugal classifiers because numerical cues were converted to binary cues, and the classifier was limited to using the six cues selected by Basic Tallying. The other version of logistic regression used numerical cues as given and also used ridge regularization, a statistical approach designed to prevent overfitting. In each environment, we used out-of-sample testing and assigned 30 percent of the instances to the test set. We varied the number of training instances, starting from just a few to as many as the environment allows but no more than five thousand.

Figure 3.9 portrays the results. The figure shows out-of-sample balanced accuracy (mean of hit rate and correct rejection rate) for different training set sizes. We can categorize the results into three cases.

In the first case, all algorithms show about the same performance. This holds for predicting whether a Broadway show will survive more than six months, and whether the corroboree frog is present in the Snowy Mountains. Here the three fast-and-frugal classifiers predict equally well, and on par with logistic regression and ridge regression. This similarity in performance holds across the entire range of training set size.

In the second case, the three fast-and-frugal classifiers show similar performance for smaller training set sizes, but for larger sizes the Basic Fast-and-Frugal Tree trails behind. That result holds for determining digits from images and for deciding whether an SMS is spam. In classifying SMS, all three fast-and-frugal classifiers perform better than logistic regression, and for classifying digits, the best fast-and-frugal classifier matches logistic regression. For both digits and SMS, ridge regression performs best for larger training set sizes. Ridge regression has at its disposal 784 (28 × 28) cues for identifying digits, and 1,418 cues for classifying SMS, compared to only 6, or even 3, cues for the fast-and-frugal classifiers. Ridge regression also uses the exact numerical cue values. What is astounding is that, being restricted

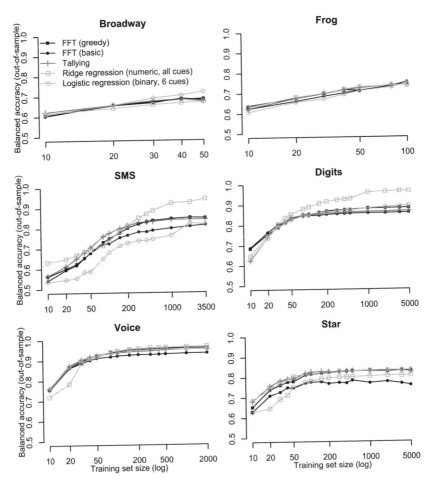

Figure 3.9
The out-of-sample balanced accuracy of fast-and-frugal classifiers. Balanced accuracy of logistic regression is shown as a baseline in two versions. See text for details. "FFT" stands for fast-and-frugal tree.

to only six pixels, the fast-and-frugal classifiers can make good predictions at all. It turns out that the fast-and-frugal classifiers determine whether a digit is a 9 or a 4 on the basis of the shape of the digit: if the top is completely closed, then it is a 9; otherwise it is a 4.

In the third case, the best fast-and-frugal classifiers predict as accurately as the best regression model, but with more variance between algorithms than in the first case. Here ridge regression and the Basic Fast-and-Frugal Tree trail some percentage points behind the other algorithms. That holds for classifying a voice as female or male, and for determining whether a space observation is of a galaxy.

These results provide a general insight: none of the algorithms always predicts best. The four environments where the best fast-and-frugal classifier matches the accuracy of the best regression model have in common that the number of cues is relatively small, between seven (Broadway) and twenty (voice). In contrast, the two cases where ridge regression excels are characterized by a very large number of cues together with large training set sizes.

3.7 Fast-and-Frugal Trees and Signal Detection Theory

Consider a fast-and-frugal tree with three cues that have already been ordered. Depending on the problem, we might want a tree that generates few misses or one that generates few false alarms. How can we build trees that achieve a desired balance? The answer lies in the structure of exits. A fast-and-frugal tree with three cues has four exits. The two exits at the bottom level of the tree are given. This leaves the designer with two choices: where to place the exit at the top level of the tree and where to place the exit at the second level of the tree. Because each one of these two exits has two possible locations, there are four possible exit structures, defining four fast-and-frugal trees.

Figure 3.10 shows four fast-and-frugal trees that we describe in this book. They all have three cues but differ in their exit structure. To make the trees comparable, we use the term *signal* for the positive class, such as coronary care unit, and the term *noise* for the negative class, such a regular nursing bed. The tree on the leftmost side has the structure of the bail-or-jail tree from chapter 1. Both of its two top exits are set to signal (jail), meaning that the chance of a miss is minimized. To its right, the second tree has the structure of the coronary care tree. Its top exit is again set to signal, but its second exit is set to noise, meaning that it will have more misses but fewer false alarms (than if it had the exit structure of the bail-or-jail tree). The next tree to the right has a top exit set to noise and the second exit set to signal. It thus has more misses but fewer false alarms (than if it had the exit structure of the coronary care tree). This tree is designed for soldiers who

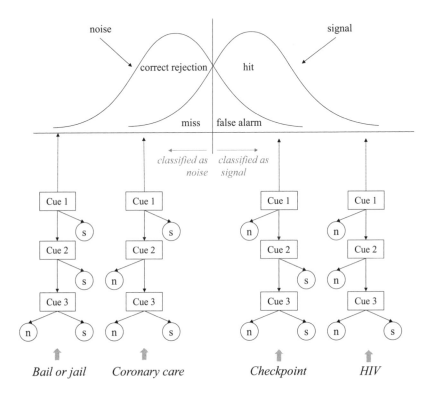

Figure 3.10
The relationship between fast-and-frugal trees and signal detection theory.

need to classify vehicles approaching a military checkpoint as hostile or not (we analyze this tree in chapter 6). The issue at checkpoints is to avoid shooting at civilians, that is, to avoid false alarms. Finally, the rightmost tree has the structure of the HIV tree from chapter 1. Both of its top two exits are set to noise. Thus the chance of a false alarm is minimized.

The figure illustrates how to choose the exits of a fast-and-frugal tree, depending on what is more important to avoid: misses or false alarms.[12] Additionally it shows that, for a fast-and-frugal tree with only a few cues, the trade-off between misses and false alarms does not need to be precisely estimated by a numerical parameter. Choosing one of four trees is enough. Even if four cues had been used, we would have only eight possible fast-and-frugal trees to choose from.

The four trees of figure 3.10 map to four points in ROC space. The classic theory that generates ROC curves is shown at the top of figure 3.10. Known as *signal detection theory*, it assumes two classes, signal and noise, and normal distributions of the instances in each class.[13] Notably, the distributions overlap, meaning that we have no way to make perfect classifications. The vertical line is the threshold according to which classifications are made and is adjustable. Each of the four trees corresponds to a different threshold value.

This analysis shows how one can understand the relationship between fast-and-frugal classifiers and so-called optimal classifiers. An "optimal" classifier such as one derived from signal detection theory—which is equivalent to Neyman-Pearson statistical theory—needs to make assumptions such as normal distributions and a single continuous variable separating the two classes. In the wild, it is by definition impossible to know whether such assumptions will hold in the present or in the future. An "optimal" classifier is optimal only relative to its assumptions and does not necessarily lead to an optimal classification in the wild. For instance, even in out-of-sample prediction, fast-and-frugal trees can predict better than signal detection theory.[14]

3.8 Ecological Rationality

By definition, in the wild no way exists to determine the classifier that will lead to optimal results in the future. Nevertheless, it is possible to specify conditions under which one classifier will lead to better, similar, or worse results than another classifier. To find these conditions is the topic of the study of *ecological rationality*.[15] The term *ecological* refers to the idea of evaluating the rationality of strategies in general, and classifiers in particular, in relation to the structure of the environment at hand.

Relation between Tallying and Fast-and-Frugal Trees

The bail-or-jail tree is a fast-and-frugal tree containing reasons to send defendants to jail. But the tree can also be represented as a tallying rule: if at least one reason is in place, send the defendant to jail; otherwise grant bail. With k cues, the general result is the following:

> *Any tallying rule with a threshold of 1 or* k *can be represented as a fast-and-frugal tree. And any fast-and-frugal tree that sets all exits (except one exit at the bottom) to "signal" or all exits (except one exit at the bottom) to "noise" can be represented as a tallying rule.*

In other words, a fast-and-frugal tree in which the order of cues does not matter for making a classification is equivalent to a tallying rule. Consider

figure 3.7. These two fast-and-frugal trees are located on the rightmost and leftmost sides. This observation leads to another result:

In a tallying rule, setting the threshold to 1 or k *minimizes misses or false alarms, respectively, instead of balancing the two kinds of errors.*

Thus, tallying and fast-and-frugal trees, using the same cues and cue directions, become identical when they aim to minimize either misses or false alarms.

When Is a Single Cue as Good as a Complex Classifier?

Consider a company that wants to predict which of its hundreds of thousands of customers will buy from it again. The company intends to send targeted offers or catalogs, without wasting money on previous customers who will not buy in the future. Thus the classification problem entails deciding whether a customer is "active" or "inactive." Experienced managers report that they use a classification rule with a single cue, as in the following heuristic.[16]

Hiatus heuristic: If a customer has not bought anything within the last nine months, classify as inactive; otherwise classify as active.

The rule is fast and frugal compared with standard models of marketing, such as the Pareto/NBD (negative binomial distribution) model or logistic regression. Studies have shown that the hiatus heuristic leads to more accurate predictions "out-of-population" than these and other complex strategies do. For an airline, the heuristic made 77 percent correct predictions of future purchases, while the Pareto/NBD model achieved only 74 percent.[17] For an apparel business, the values were 83 percent versus 75 percent. These algorithms were trained on forty weeks of data and used to predict customer purchases in the subsequent forty weeks. This is an example of out-of-population prediction about an unknown future. A follow-up study with twenty-four businesses replicated this less-is-more effect in out-of-population prediction. On average, the hiatus heuristic made more correct predictions than random forests and logistic regression, as well as the Pareto/NBD, all of which used more cues.[18]

The question of ecological rationality is: can we find conditions under which we can prove that a classifier such as the hiatus heuristic with a single cue can match or outperform classifiers that use the same cue and more (and vice versa)? Consider a linear classifier with k binary cues, $x_i = 0$ or 1, where $i = 1, 2, \ldots, k$, that classifies a customer as active if

$$\sum_{i=1}^{k} w_i x_i \geq h, \text{where } w_i \geq 0, i = 1, \ldots, k.$$

In other words, all cues are weighted and then summed up; if the sum is equal to or larger than a threshold h, then the prediction is "active." Here is an intuitive condition called the *dominant cue condition*:[19]

$$w_1 \geq h > \sum_{i=2}^{k} w_i.$$

Let *single cue* refer to the cue with the largest weight (x_1). The condition says that the weight of the single cue is at least as large as the threshold h and that h is in turn larger than the sum of all other cue weights. If this condition holds, then the single cue classifies in the same way as the linear classifier. Here is why. Imagine that you are adding the contribution of each cue one by one, starting with the single cue. If a cue has value 1, its contribution is the cue weight. If a cue has value 0, its contribution is 0. If the single cue has value 1, then its contribution is w_1, and the threshold has already been reached (because $w_1 \geq h$). The instance can then be classified as "active" without needing to compute the contributions from the other cues. If, on the other hand, the single cue has value 0, then its contribution is 0, and the threshold cannot be reached even if all other cues have value 1 (because $\sum_{i=2}^{k} w_i < h$). In both cases, the other cues are irrelevant and can be ignored.

The dominant cue condition explains how a single cue, such as the hiatus heuristic, can make decisions identical to those of a more complex rule while requiring less information and less computation.

When Is a Fast-and-Frugal Tree as Good as a Complex Classifier?

The dominant cue condition holds for a single cue but can be generalized to fast-and-frugal trees.[20] The condition needs to hold not only for the top cue but for each cue. That is, every cue i needs to dominate all other cues whose weight is smaller than the weight of cue i. This is called the *noncompensatory cues* condition because a cue cannot be compensated ("overthrown") by cues whose weights are smaller:

$$w_i \geq \sum_{j=i+1}^{k} w_j, \text{ for all } j = 1, \ldots \ k-1.$$

The noncompensatory cues condition explains how a fast-and-frugal tree can make decisions identical to those of a more complex rule while requiring less information and less computation. This is because when the condition holds, the fast-and-frugal tree classifies in the same way as the linear classifier.[21]

The Bias-Variance Dilemma

The two conditions, dominant cue and noncompensatory cues, explain conditions under which a linear strategy, using more cues and computation, leads to the same decisions as those made by fast-and-frugal classifiers. However, they do not explain situations where the fast-and-frugal classifiers predict even more accurately than a linear strategy. For situations of out-of-sample prediction, the bias-variance dilemma can offer explanatory help. Although it was formulated for a different kind of problem from the one studied here,[22] it can nevertheless provide some insights.[23]

Consider a problem of estimating an unknown variable, where samples are repeatedly drawn from the same population. For each sample, the prediction method in question produces an estimate; the average squared difference between the estimates and the true value is called the *total prediction error* of the algorithm. This error can be decomposed as follows:[24]

Total error = (bias)^2 + variance + irreducible error.

The bias of an algorithm is defined as the difference between the algorithm's average estimate and the true value, and the variance is the variation of these estimates around their average. The bias term relates to how well the functional form of the classifier can represent reality. For instance, if the true state of the world is a parabola, and the model used is linear, then the model has a bias. On the other hand, if the true state is linear and the model is a parabola, then the model has no bias, because a parabola can represent a straight line. However, if the parameters of the parabola and of the linear model are estimated from training examples, the parabola will have more variance than the linear model does. The reason is that the parabola is more flexible than a linear model and can easily adjust itself to the idiosyncrasies of the training data.

When a single cue can make as accurate decisions as a more complex model, these two classifiers share the same bias. The two conditions mentioned earlier refer to the bias component of the error only, saying that if they hold, fast-and-frugal classifiers and linear models have the same bias.[25] Prediction also involves an additional source of error, called *variance*. Variance increases with the number and kind of free parameters and decreases with training set size. A fast-and-frugal classifier that has no free parameters, as in the case of the hiatus heuristic with a fixed hiatus, thus does not produce error from variance, only from bias. If the bias of the heuristic is the same as that of more complex models, but the complex models incur further error owing to variance, then one can anticipate situations where the simple classifier can predict more accurately than complex models. Even if the bias is larger, the total error can still be lower for the heuristic classifier because of savings in variance. In these cases, less is more.

4 Classification in Machine Learning

If robots do everything, then what are we going to do?
—a five-year-old in a Beijing kindergarten

The study of fast-and-frugal heuristics begins with the observation that humans are very good at classification and proposes classification rules that are based on people's core capacities. For example, fast-and-frugal trees are built on the basic principle of ordering, and tallying on that of counting.

Machine learning asks how a computer can make accurate classifications. It is based on data, clever algorithms, and heavy computational power rather than on human intuition and capacities and may result in complex classification rules. Deep neural networks employed in facial recognition can be accurate, but they are not transparent. Random forests, another classifier widely used in machine learning, produces classification rules that often comprise hundreds or thousands of decision trees, which are also not transparent.

The study of fast-and-frugal heuristics places a value on transparency of the classification rule. Transparency is important in machine learning as well, especially when algorithms make decisions that affect people. Nevertheless, simple and transparent rules are often ignored in favor of complex ones, even when the simple rule is equally (or more) accurate. As we will see, Google tried to predict the spread of the flu with big data analytics without testing its algorithm against simpler rules that ultimately perform better.

4.1   What Is Machine Learning?

Machine learning is a scientific discipline that studies how computer programs can improve their performance by learning from observations of the world. It is one of the most promising approaches to achieving artificial intelligence. Among the various approaches to machine learning are supervised, unsupervised, and reinforcement learning.

Classification is a supervised learning problem. In supervised learning, an algorithm learns the association between the cues and a characteristic of an instance, such as its class. An example is the classification of moles into harmless skin conditions or dangerous melanomas. By observing a collection of moles, the algorithm can use the relationship between the moles' cues, such as size, color, and texture, and the moles' class as diagnosed in a biopsy to learn a classification rule.

In unsupervised learning, an algorithm uses the characteristics of an instance to infer the structure of a data set but does not assign instances to classes. A typical unsupervised learning task is to cluster the observations into groups such that the observations in one group are more similar to one another than to the observations in the other groups. For example, a clustering algorithm might group moles according to their visual appearance. These clusters may help doctors gain insight into the nature of moles.

Supervised learning and unsupervised learning map onto the two common definitions of classification given in chapter 1. The first, the act of determining a classification rule for a given set of classes, is a supervised learning task and is the focus of this book. The second, the act of determining a set of classes, that is, developing a taxonomy, is an unsupervised learning task.

Reinforcement learning enables a computer to learn how to perform a sequential task such as driving a car or playing chess. The computer learns through trial and error, by observing the consequences of its own actions. For example, a computer can learn how to play chess by playing the game with itself (or with other opponents) and observing at the end of each game whether the game was a win, loss, or draw.

We now discuss three successful machine learning applications, two in supervised learning and one in reinforcement learning. What all three applications have in common is that the machine learning models are trained on extremely large amounts of data in a stable environment.

4.2 Successes of Machine Learning

Face Recognition

One successful application of supervised machine learning is automated face recognition. Smartphone users can unlock their phone in less than a second by holding it in front of their face. Online social networks automatically name one's friends in a photograph. Border controls around the world use automated systems to compare people's faces with their passport pictures to increase the speed of entrance and to reduce personnel. In China, the use of face recognition is ubiquitous: it is used to check identities at ATMs, to check in at a hotel, and to identify drivers who use ride-sharing services.[1]

In 2015, Google reported a milestone success in automated face recognition.[2] Google's algorithm was a deep artificial neural network trained on more than 100 million photographs of eight million people. It inferred the faces from red, green, and blue values of the 50,176 pixels of each color photograph, resulting in 150,528 cues. The structure of the neural network was complex, with 7.6 million free parameters. These parameters were estimated in more than one thousand hours of training time on a network of powerful computers. After training, the task was to infer whether two photographs of faces show the same person. Faces shown to the neural network during this test differed from those on which the network was trained. The neural network was accurate in 99.6 percent of the cases. For the same set of pictures, human participants in an experiment were correct in 99.2 percent of the cases.[3]

Automated face recognition can be effective in the real world. Smartphone owners will almost always successfully use face recognition to unlock their phone at the first attempt, whereas a pickpocket who tries to unlock a stolen phone will rarely succeed.

The technology is also being used for state surveillance and criminal investigation. In 2014, China's State Council announced the creation of a surveillance system that is "omnipresent, fully networked, always working and fully controllable."[4] By 2018, the government had installed some 200 million surveillance video cameras. The cameras aim to track passersby continuously, detect problematic behavior, and identify relationships among people. These data are combined with hotel, flight, and train records and data on social media accounts to form a social credit score for every citizen, rewarding the "well-behaved" and punishing the others. For instance, citizens who have low scores may not be allowed to buy plane tickets or use fast trains, and their children might be excluded from the best schools. Because the scores of one's friends may influence one's own score, people unfriend potentially low-scoring friends on social media. According to Human Rights Watch, potential targets of this integrated surveillance system include ethnic and religious minorities, as well as political activists.[5]

Two important applications of face recognition are *screening* and *identification*. This distinction is well known in health care. Mammography can be applied to women without or with symptoms. In the first case, doctors use it for screening, and in the second case for identification (diagnosis). If a mammogram is positive, then the probability of breast cancer is much higher for a woman with symptoms than for women generally screened. The situation is analogous to surveillance. In screening, faces from the general public are compared with a database of suspects' faces. Identification, by contrast, takes place after a crime has happened; the photograph of only one or a few suspects is compared with a database of photographs. Here identification provides a reason to investigate a suspect, just as it provides reasons to investigate a woman with symptoms. In both contexts, screening leads to more false alarms.

Screening

In the UEFA Champions League final of 2017, held in Cardiff, Wales, the police screened the faces of more than 170,000 soccer fans who visited the city for the game between Real Madrid and Juventus. The face recognition system reported 2,470 matches with the criminal database of 500,000 images. However, 2,297 of these purported matches were false alarms.[6] Although, according to the police, no one was wrongly arrested, many innocent people became the focus of investigation. Face recognition screening creates more work for the police: all suspicions raised by the computer need to be reevaluated by humans.

Amazon's facial recognition system has been tested by comparing photos of the 535 members of the US Congress with twenty-five thousand photos of previously arrested individuals. The system reported twenty-eight matches, all of them false. Thus the false alarm rate was 28/535, or around 5 percent.[7]

Face recognition screening is analogous to HIV screening, discussed in chapter 1. When a large random sample of the general population takes a single ELISA test, a high number of people who do not have HIV obtain a false-positive test result.

Identification

Consider a criminal investigation by the FBI, where the police obtain a photograph of a suspect from a surveillance camera at a crime scene. To identify the suspect, the FBI employs an automatic face recognition system that compares the suspect's image with a database of 400 million photographs. Most of these photographs are not of criminals but of people from the general public whose images were collected from visa and passport databases.[8]

Identification leads to many fewer false alarms than screening. However, even in identification, the number of false alarms can be large. We do not know the actual error rate of the FBI's face recognition system. According to the FBI, if a suspect is in the bureau's picture database, the system will list the suspect among the top fifty matches in 85 percent of the cases.[9] But what happens if a suspect is not in the database? How often do innocent people get picked up and investigated?

Skin Cancer Diagnosis

Can a computer detect skin cancer more accurately than a dermatologist? In 2017, scholars from Stanford University investigated how well a deep neural network learned to detect dangerous skin cancer from 127,463 images.[10] Using three classification tasks, researchers compared the accuracy of the network with that of more than twenty dermatologists. For example, one task was to classify pictures of 33 malignant melanomas and 97 benign lesions, as measured by a biopsy. Neither the doctors nor the neural network had seen these images before the test. In all three classification tasks, the algorithm performed better than the average dermatologist. On the other hand, in each task, some dermatologists performed as well as, or even slightly better than, the neural network. But on the whole, the deep-learning approach performed impressively. Moreover, the neural network could potentially be made available on the smartphones of the general public, allowing for regular automated and thus cheap skin cancer screening for everyone.[11]

In this study, however, the dermatologists were working at a disadvantage. In a real-world clinical setting, the dermatologist looks at the skin itself, not at a picture of it. A dermatologist can also interact with the patient.

Beyond comparing performance alone, a much larger question emerges. Would the impressive success of deep learning actually save lives? The evidence does not support that idea. First, it is not even clear whether skin cancer screening is generally beneficial. The US Preventive Services Task Force does not recommend screening at this time, having concluded in 2016 that "the current evidence is insufficient to assess the balance of benefits and harms of visual skin examination by a clinician to screen for skin cancer in adults."[12] Second, imagine that a deep-learning algorithm is able to predict the result of a biopsy correctly in 100 percent of cases. Would that benefit patients? The medical researcher Gilbert Welch and colleagues showed that the rate of skin biopsies increased 2.5-fold between 1986 and 2001 in the United States, and the number of diagnosed melanoma increased 2.4-fold.[13] The mortality from melanoma, however, did not change over the years. The authors conclude that the growing number of screenings increased the rate of overdiagnosis: cancers that would not have harmed or killed the patient were more frequently detected and unnecessarily treated. Third, randomized studies showed a reduction in cancer-specific mortality for only a few cancer screenings, including mammography for breast cancer and sigmoidoscopy for colorectal cancer; skin cancer is not one of them.[14] And if one looks not just at cancer-specific mortality but at the general mortality, none of these screenings have been shown to save lives. If no cure exists for a particular cancer, then diagnosing it early does not save lives. Instead all screenings can harm patients by creating false alarms and introducing unnecessary worries. Thus the remarkable diagnostic capability of the deep-learning system does not automatically benefit patients.

AlphaZero

Another milestone of machine learning is the 3:0 victory of the computer program AlphaGo in May 2017 over Ke Jie, the world's top-ranked Go player at the time. Go is a traditional Chinese board game that has been considered extremely challenging to master for computer programs. The complexity of Go makes it impossible to exhaustively enumerate all possible moves: a player can make roughly 250 legal moves per position in Go, compared with around 35 in chess. Like Google's face recognition algorithm,

AlphaGo uses a deep neural network to play the game. Learning to play Go is a reinforcement learning task. AlphaGo does not learn to classify a potential move as good or bad independently of the previous and next possible moves but instead learns how to win the game with a sequence of moves. Whereas previous versions of the algorithm learned from games played by human experts, the new-generation AlphaGo Zero is able to learn via the rules of the game only, without any further human input. All it does is use trial and error by playing millions of games against itself.[15]

Just a few months later, in December 2017, a third-generation algorithm, AlphaZero, was introduced.[16] It beat not only AlphaGo Zero at Go but also the best chess and shogi (also known as Japanese chess) computer programs at the respective games. This neural network was trained on each of the three games individually by playing from 24 to 140 million games against itself. Its architecture was not tailored to each game but remained the same across all three.

AlphaGo, AlphaGo Zero, and AlphaZero play in the lab, not in the wild. Successes of machine learning—compared with human performance—are most pronounced in situations that are well-defined and stable, such as games. For example, Go has clear and fixed rules. Even the visual pattern of skin cancer is relatively the same from patient to patient. Faces do change with age, but only very slowly, and smartphones that use face recognition deal with this problem by updating the image of their owner from time to time.

In general, as said in the introduction, our thesis—the unstable-world principle—is that the more stable a situation is, the more likely machine learning is to outperform humans. If stability does not exist, then humans and fast-and-frugal classification rules can have an advantage.

4.3 Failures of Machine Learning

Google Flu Trends

Influenza, commonly known as "the flu," is a major cause of death worldwide. The World Health Organization estimates that three to five million people are infected every year and 290,000 to 650,000 die from it.[17] The prevalence of the flu varies with the season and peaks in winter.

Figure 4.1 shows the proportion of doctor visits related to the flu in the United States for all weeks in a decade. The dotted vertical lines mark the first week in a year. The seasonal pattern is pronounced, but the peaks differ between years, both in their height and in the week of occurrence. In some years, several peaks can be observed.

Predicting the occurrence of the flu and taking mitigating actions can reduce its spread.[18] The data shown in the figure seem a useful source for monitoring flu outbreaks. But these data—collected by the US Centers for Disease Control and Prevention—become available only one to two weeks after the doctor visits, which does not allow real-time detection of the spread of the flu.

In 2008, Google launched Google Flu Trends for real-time detection of flu outbreaks in the United States. Underlying this algorithm is the intuition that users infected by the flu will use Google as a search engine for diagnosing their symptoms and seeking treatment and advice. The researchers at Google identified search queries that correlated highly with flu-related doctor visits. Google Flu Trends used forty-five of these queries as cues in a linear model.

Initially, Google Flu Trends was trained on data from 2003 to 2007 and tested on data from 2007 to 2008.[19] In both fitting and prediction, the model performed well. In 2009, however, Google Flu Trends failed to predict the outbreak of the swine flu, which was the first influenza pandemic since the Russian flu in 1977.[20] As is often the case, if a complex model fails, it is made even more complex: Google revised its model in autumn 2009

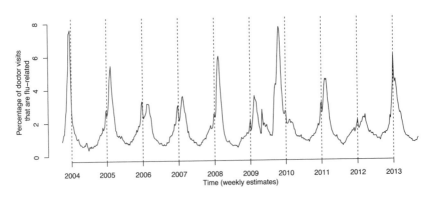

Figure 4.1
Weekly percentage of doctor visits in the United States that are flu related. The data were collected by the US Centers for Disease Control and Prevention.

by inflating the number of cues from 45 to 160.[21] But this version fared poorly in prediction, as well.[22] From August 2011 to September 2013, the new model overestimated the proportion of flu-related doctor visits in 100 out of 108 weeks.[23] In 2015, Google Flu Trends was shut down.

Why Did Google Flu Trends Fail?

One major reason for the failure of Google Flu Trends is that the flu is not a stable phenomenon but constantly undergoes changes. For instance, the swine flu of 2009 differed from the seasonal flu in several ways.[24] In the United States, the first cases of the swine flu were reported in April, and the outbreak peaked in October, whereas the seasonal flu typically starts in October and peaks between December and February. Also, the swine flu had additional symptoms such as diarrhea and vomiting. Unlike the seasonal flu, the swine flu's infection rate was lower for older people, indicating a preexisting immunity to the virus. These differences are likely to be reflected in different search queries by Google users and can at least partially explain the failure of the algorithm to predict the outbreak.

Another source of failure can be traced to changes made by Google itself. Its engineers constantly tried to fine-tune the search algorithm, in reaction to which users used different search queries.[25] For example, in 2012, Google users searching for medical symptoms saw an additional box on the search results page listing potential diagnoses. This could have influenced their search behavior. The behavior of Google users is also affected by the media. Press reports on the flu or related topics can trigger flu-related searches by people who do not have any symptoms but are simply curious. The algorithm cannot distinguish between these users and those with actual symptoms.

Another problem lies in the development of the Google Flu Trends algorithm. To train the model, the correlations of 50 million search terms with flu-related doctor visits were evaluated, and only the forty-five search terms with the highest correlation were incorporated into the first version of the algorithm. The correlations were computed by using 128 weekly estimates in nine regions of the United States. This training sample of 1,152 data points is small in comparison with the 50 million potential cues. One might expect that some of these correlations are high, even if they have no structural relationship to the flu. For example, Google reports that "high school basketball" has one of the one hundred highest correlations with flu-related doctor visits.[26] The reason is that high school basketball and the flu have similar seasons, starting in November and ending in March.[27]

Can Simple Rules Do Better Than Big Data?

When the first Google Flu Trends algorithm failed, its engineers had a choice of how to revise the algorithm. They followed the heuristic "If you have a complex problem and your complex algorithm fails, make the algorithm even more complex." We propose an alternative heuristic: "If you are dealing with deep uncertainty and your algorithm fails, make it simpler." In what follows, we show how to proceed in this alternative way.

Psychological research indicates that in situations of change and disruption, people rely on recency. In 1838, Thomas Brown had already formulated the law of recency, which states that recent experiences come to mind more easily than those from the distant past and are often the sole information that guides human decisions.[28] More contemporary research has reported that an exponential relationship exists between the time since the last event (e.g., a particular word occurring in a *New York Times* headline or in an email communication) and the probability that the event will occur in the next time interval (e.g., one day later), and people do not rely blindly on recency but adapt to the statistical structure of the environment.[29] In the spirit of this research, we developed the following simple rule.

Recency heuristic: Predict that this week's flu-related doctor visits will equal those of the most recent data, from two weeks ago.

Unlike the Google Flu Trends algorithm, which is calibrated on four full years of data, the recency heuristic ignores this information and takes on only the most recent data point. It can thus react to unexpected changes quickly. We tested the recency heuristic using the same data on which the revised Google Flu Trends algorithm was tested, namely, weekly observations between September 2009 and September 2013. The result of the comparison between these two approaches is shown in table 4.1. The revised Google Flu Trends algorithm had a mean absolute error of 0.49 percentage points over the four years. Although this error might seem small, one can see in figure 4.1 that the percentage of flu-related doctor visits ranged between 1 percent and 8 percent, with a mean of 1.8 percent. Therefore, a naive prediction of 0 percent across all observations would lead to a mean absolute error of just 1.8 percentage points.

The recency heuristic had a mean absolute error of only 0.33 percentage points. It is derived from psychological principles of how people make predictions when things change. The heuristic does not analyze millions of search terms, look for statistical correlations, or test hundreds of thousands of models. Its predictions can be made in an instant because its single cue is easily accessible within seconds from the website of the Centers for Disease Control and Prevention.[30] And, unlike the secret Google algorithms, the heuristic is absolutely transparent.

A statistically minded person might now interject: "Why don't you make a regression out of this single cue? That would allow you to be more flexible and adapt the parameters every week." Researchers have in fact followed the regression approach. The data scientist David Lazer and colleagues showed that a two-parameter regression, where the parameters were the weight of the recency cue (which they call two-week lag) and an intercept, had an average absolute error of 0.34 percentage points.[31] This approach gives us no improvement over the recency heuristic. Furthermore, the recency heuristic has no free parameters that need to be estimated, entails no computation, and can be easily applied. In contrast, the parameters of the regression need to be updated every week.

Table 4.1

A simple heuristic leads to less error in predicting flu-related doctor visits than does Google's big data analytics

	Cues	Mean absolute error in prediction (percentage points)
Google Flu Trends (revised version of 2009)	160 cues selected from 50 million search terms	0.49
Two-parameter regression (with flu-related doctor visits two weeks ago)	Single cue	0.34
Recency heuristic (zero free parameters)	Single cue	0.33

The table shows the performance of the second Google Flu Trends model, updated after its failure to predict the swine flu in the summer of 2009. The predictions refer to the period from September 2009 to September 2013. Predictive accuracy is measured as the mean absolute difference between predictions and observations.

Predicting flu-related doctor visits is a problem not of out-of-sample but of out-of-population prediction. In an out-of-sample test, one would have used all the data about doctor visits between, say, 2009 and 2013 and randomly assigned these to two sets, using one for training and the other for testing. In contrast, the task here was to predict new visits in the future. As we saw in the case of the swine flu, the future was unlike the past.

In the wild, a single good reason can be more useful than big data.[32] One general lesson is that one should always compare the performance of a complex algorithm to fast-and-frugal classifiers. Google's researchers did not follow this insight and did not compare their model to simple rules that do not need big data from search engines.

DNA Testing

You might think that a DNA test is an error-free method for identifying criminals. This is not true. A match between the evidence (the DNA sample found at a crime scene) and a suspect's DNA does not prove that the suspect is guilty. Nor does it prove that the suspect has even been at the crime scene. The genetic materials could have been planted at the crime scene by someone else, mislabeled, or contaminated in the laboratory. Even if presence at the crime scene is established, the suspect could have been there before or after the crime. These and other uncertainties are discussed in detail in the book *Calculated Risk: How to Know When Numbers Deceive You*.[33] The uncertainty we focus on here is the uncertainty inherent in the outcome of the DNA test.

The metric reflecting the uncertainty of a DNA test is the *likelihood ratio*. It is the ratio of the probability of match between the suspect's DNA sample and the DNA sample found at the crime scene to the same probability for a random person. If a DNA sample is complete and not contaminated, the likelihood ratio is often estimated to be between one million and one billion.[34]

But what if the genetic samples are of lesser quality? Tiny, incomplete genetic samples and mixtures of genetic material from several people are frequently the only available DNA information at crime scenes. In the 1980s and 1990s, DNA testing was limited to complete samples from semen, blood, and saliva, but with advances in technology, laboratories started to analyze genetic material of lesser quality.

The DNA laboratory in the office of New York City's chief medical examiner developed a forensic statistical tool (FST) to analyze these challenging DNA samples. This tool was put into practice in 2011 and soon became popular within and beyond the borders of New York City. It claimed to require only twenty trillionths of a gram of genetic material to test whether DNA samples match.

The use of FST in courtrooms was controversial because its algorithm was proprietary; it was not made public. In several cases, the defense tried in vain to gain access to the source code. Not until June 2016 was an expert in forensic software given the opportunity to analyze the algorithm for the defense in a case of illegal possession of a weapon. According to the *New York Times*, he and other experts familiar with the underlying algorithm questioned the accuracy of FST.[35] Several of its assumptions are incorrect and can lead to inaccurate predictions. For example, FST does not take into account that relatives in a mixture (i.e., DNA sample stemming from several people) share DNA. Furthermore, the algorithm cannot accurately determine the number of people contributing to the mixture and does not factor in that genetic evidence is degraded by time and weather.

FST is not a transparent tool. Most of the lab workers who applied the algorithm did not understand it and could not check whether it led to potentially wrongful convictions resulting from violations of its assumptions. In September 2016, New York City stopped using FST.

FST is not the only DNA testing software facing problems. For example, in a murder trial in 2016, the two commercial forensic algorithms TrueAllele and STRmix reached opposite conclusions regarding the match between a defendant's DNA and the DNA found at the crime scene.[36]

The failures of Google Flu Trends and FST have two things in common. First, both failed to deal with the uncertainty of flu and crime. In the case of Google Flu Trends, the uncertainty lies in the instability in the environment. Search queries by users, characteristics of the flu, and the search engine itself change over time. In DNA testing, the uncertainty lies in the quality of the data, that is, in the tiny and contaminated DNA samples. Second, neither algorithm is transparent. Google did not report all search terms that were incorporated in its model, and the proprietary forensic algorithm returned only a probability estimate, without providing any insight into how it was calculated. Making an algorithm transparent could protect against failure because its assumptions can be verified or questioned.

4.4 Transparency of Machine Learning Models

In May 2018, the General Data Protection Regulation went into effect in the European Union. It mainly regulates data protection but also restricts the use of automated decision making on personal issues such as getting credit or insurance. The regulation states the right of citizens to access "meaningful information about the logic involved, as well as the significance and the envisaged consequences" of the algorithms. In other words, it requires that EU citizens be told how an algorithm makes a decision based on their personal data.[37]

The regulation has spawned a heated debate. On the one hand, some experts suggested that a strict regulation would make "deep learning illegal."[38] On the other hand, some voices consider the EU regulation to be too vague to change the data industry.

What can be done? We see two issues concerning lack of transparency that need to be addressed. The first is secrecy for proprietary reasons. The second is algorithmic complexity, as in the case of deep neural networks. Most algorithms used by credit scorers, courts, and other institutions that score people are not neural networks but linear algorithms. Consequently, the German Advisory Council for Consumer Affairs recommended that credit scorers and others reveal to the public the cues used and their weights.[39] This would allow individuals to understand why, for instance, they were denied a loan or bail (see chap. 1). More and more, the machine learning community is beginning to treat transparency as a virtue on par with accuracy and has increased its efforts to provide "interpretable" algorithms.[40]

Unfortunately, most machine learning algorithms are not transparent to most people. Deep neural networks are not interpretable, despite ongoing efforts. Another successful yet not interpretable algorithm is random forest, which is a collection of many—often hundreds—of decision trees. The prediction of the forest is the "majority vote" of all trees; how it comes about is not intuitive.[41]

One solution to the problem of complex, nontransparent algorithms is simple algorithms that are as accurate. Transparent machine learning algorithms do exist, and we investigate how fast-and-frugal trees and tallying relate to some of them.

4.5   Fast-and-Frugal Trees and Machine Learning

Decision Trees

On April 10, 1912, the luxury ocean liner *Titanic* left Southampton on its maiden voyage across the Atlantic to New York City. Just four days later, it collided with an iceberg and sank within three hours. The ship was carrying more than 2,200 passengers, only 711 of whom survived.[42] Did every passenger have the same chance to survive, or did the rescue operation favor the rich over the poor, or vice versa?

Figure 4.2 (left panel) shows a tree induced by CART, a prominent machine learning algorithm.[43] CART, which stands for *classification and regression tree*, was published back in 1984 and is still widely used today. We describe it in detail later. The first question in the tree is whether the passenger was male. If no, then the second question is whether she was traveling third class. If yes, then she is classified as dead, otherwise as having survived. In other words, all females who traveled first or second class are categorized as survivors. If the passenger was male, however, then the second question is whether he was an adult. If yes, then he is classified as dead. If the passenger was a boy, then the question is whether he traveled

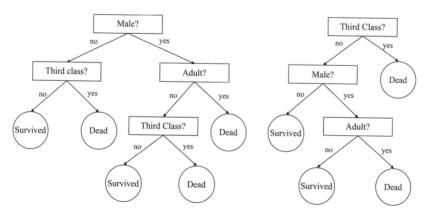

Figure 4.2

Decision tree (*left*) and fast-and-frugal tree (*right*) classifying whether a passenger on the *Titanic* survived or died.

third class. If yes, dead; if no, survived. Male passengers are predicted to have survived only if a boy and not in third class, while traveling third class means dying irrespective of gender. All in all, this tree reproduces the fate of 79 percent of the passengers correctly.

The right-hand panel in figure 4.2 shows a fast-and-frugal tree. This fast-and-frugal tree was induced by using the Best Fit method (chap. 3). It has fewer questions and exits than the CART. It is simpler, more elegant, and easier to memorize. The fast-and-frugal tree makes the same classifications as the CART. In the fast-and-frugal tree, the first question is whether the passenger traveled third class, and if so, then the passenger is classified as dead. If not, the second question is whether the passenger was male. If not, survived. Otherwise a third question is asked: whether the passenger was an adult. If yes, dead; if it is a boy, survived.

The point of the *Titanic* exercise is that machine learning has a long tradition of constructing decision trees, exemplified by CART, that are relatively transparent in comparison with neural networks. Fast-and-frugal trees are a special category of decision trees that are even more transparent than CART. They achieve transparency by enforcing a strict structure on the tree, with a decision at each level and a limited number of levels. As the example shows, CART has no mechanism to guarantee picking the most transparent tree.

Constructing Decision Trees

The first algorithm to learn a decision tree was published in 1963 under the name *automatic interaction detection*.[44] It already used the key feature of today's algorithms: building a decision tree is decomposed into local problems of finding questions that minimize impurity. As defined in chapter 3, impurity measures how well a question separates two classes. Consider the first question in the CART tree (fig. 4.2). If gender were useless for classifying survivors, then the proportion of survivors among the males would be the same as among the females, that is, 32 percent in each case (711 of 2,201). Such a useless cue would be the one with the highest impurity. In fact, the gender question is the most useful because it minimizes impurity: 73 percent of the female passengers, but only 21 percent of the male passengers, survived. In the next step, the male passengers are separated into adults and children, as this is the least impure question. CART uses Gini impurity (chap. 3). Recall that, for each exit, Gini impurity is defined as $2p(1-p)$, where p is the proportion of one of two classes in this exit.

The procedure of locally finding the best split is called *greedy* (chap. 3). Whereas theoretically greedy splits do not guarantee that the most accurate tree is found, they often lead to reasonably accurate solutions.

A main reason for the popularity of CART is its effective pruning technique that reduces the size of the tree to make it less susceptible to overfitting. Pruning also makes a tree more interpretable. CART creates a provisional tree that is very large before it prunes the weakest questions. The strength of each question is determined by the extent to which Gini impurity increases if the question is deleted from the tree.

The basic fast-and-frugal trees discussed in chapter 3 strongly resemble CART. They also use Gini impurity to determine the questions. The major difference is that CART selects a tree for accuracy only, whereas fast-and-frugal trees aim for both transparency and accuracy.[45]

Flexible Models Fit Better but Predict Worse

Machine learning trees such as CART are highly flexible. Flexibility allows data to be fit well but may harm prediction. To demonstrate this, consider gerrymandering of voting districts. Imagine a world in which the votes of people depend solely on where they live, that is, on geography. There are two cues, East–West and North–South, and two parties, the Idealists and the Pragmatists. We now introduce a fairly complicated formula that separates the voters of the two parties, and then show that a CART can classify each voter without error but does not predict well.

Here is the formula of this world:

$$y = 0.5x_1 + 2x_2 - 4x_1^2 - 2x_2^2 + 2x_1x_2 + 0.5R$$

The behavior of the voters is not deterministic. In the formula, R reflects probabilistic elements in the voting behavior that follows a normal distribution with mean 0 and standard derivation 1. The values of the two cues, East–West (x_1) and North–South (x_2), range from 0 to 1. All individuals with $y > 0$ vote for the Pragmatists, the others for the Idealists. Figure 4.3 shows a picture of our world, ignoring the random component. The people who vote for the Pragmatists live mainly in the North–West, while those who vote for the Idealists live mainly in the South–East.

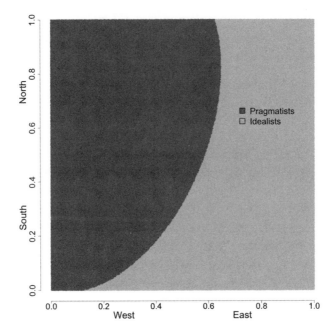

Figure 4.3
A world where geography determines voting. The impact of the probabilistic component R is not shown.

From this world, we randomly sampled five hundred voters. The top panel of figure 4.4 shows a full-grown CART tree fitted to this sample. We did not prune the tree but let it grow. This remarkable tree contains ninety-one questions, each splitting either the North–South or the East–West cue. For instance, the first question tests whether East–West < 0.56. The black exits predict Pragmatist, and the light gray exits predict Idealist. The bottom left panel shows how the tree fits to the five hundred voters. In each rectangular area, the voters are predicted to vote for the same party. No rectangle contains voters for different parties. Thus the tree fits the data perfectly (100 percent). That outcome looks impressive, but also suspicious. After all, there is randomness in our complex world.

How well, then, does this "perfect" decision tree predict? We can test this question with a new sample of five hundred voters. The bottom right panel of figure 4.4 shows the result: accuracy has dropped to 0.74.[46] Now there are

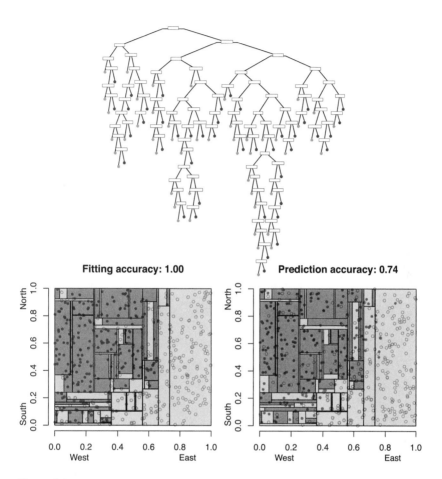

Figure 4.4

A perfect fit may not imply good prediction. The top panel shows a complex (unpruned CART) tree, which can perfectly classify voters by data fitting. A perfect fit means that each square in the bottom left panel contains only voters of one kind: black circles (Pragmatists) or light gray circles (Idealists). Black and gray circles may sometimes appear to lie on the border of the same rectangle. In these cases, the chart contains very narrow rectangles with what resemble thick lines. Identifying a tree by fitting leads to a geography that looks like gerrymandering. When it comes to predicting new voters' behavior, the tree does less well. This is overfitting, as shown in the bottom right panel.

in fact voters from different parties in the same rectangle. The perfect fit of the complex tree was an illusion. The high flexibility of the tree made it fit to the random component of the data: it *overfitted*.

The more flexible a tree, the more likely it is to overfit. One way of reducing overfitting is to introduce structures such as making the tree fast and frugal. Fast-and-frugal trees are, by definition, less flexible than unconstrained decision trees. To demonstrate this, we first used the greedy algorithm from chapter 3 to construct a complex tree that has the structure of a fast-and-frugal tree, allowing, like CART, more than one query to the same cue. This tree already overfits less and predicts better than the unpruned CART. Its accuracy in fitting and prediction is 0.85 and 0.80, respectively. The mean number of questions in the tree was 9.9 across 250 replications of our experiment. But, on average, only two questions were asked until a prediction was made.

Second, we built a fast-and-frugal tree that asks at most two questions, one for each cue (fig. 4.5, left panel). This tree achieves a fitting accuracy of 0.81 and a prediction accuracy of 0.79. Figure 4.5 (right panel) shows that it better corresponds to the true geography than does the overly complex tree in figure 4.4.

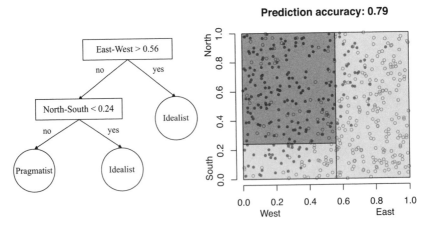

Figure 4.5
Fast-and-frugal tree that predicts how citizens will vote. The left panel shows the tree; the right panel depicts how it classifies voters in out-of-sample prediction. Simplicity does not lead to gerrymandering.

How does CART perform when employing its pruning algorithm to control the complexity of the tree in figure 4.4 (top)? It creates trees with an average of 5.7 questions and obtains a fitting and prediction accuracy of 0.84 and 0.80, meaning that it predicts about as well as the fast-and-frugal tree that asks at most two questions. Note that the CART pruning created a fast-and-frugal tree structure in 63 percent of the 250 replications.

The general lesson is that a good fit can be deceptive because of overfitting. The fast-and-frugal tree reduces overfitting by imposing a structure a priori. Typical decision tree algorithms in machine learning proceed in a different way. They do not impose a specific structure but rather use one or several of the following strategies: (1) prune a question if the classification is not substantially worse without it; (2) eliminate exits into which only few instances fall; and (3) limit the tree to a prespecified number of levels. Both approaches can be effective in resolving the problem of overfitting.

Decision Lists

In his influential book *C4.5: Programs for Machine Learning*, Ross Quinlan, a pioneer in decision tree research, wrote: "Even though the pruned trees are more compact than the originals, they can still be cumbersome, complex, and inscrutable."[47] He then proposed a method that simplifies the C4.5 tree and represents it as a decision list.

Here is a decision list for the *Titanic* problem:

If passenger was in third class, *then* dead;

else if passenger was male and an adult, *then* dead;

else passenger survived.

A *decision list* is a sequence of *if–then–else* rules.[48] If a condition holds, the rule makes a classification; otherwise the next rule is activated. In the last rule, a classification is always made.

You may have noticed that fast-and-frugal trees also have if–then–else rules. A difference is that they involve only one cue in each rule, whereas decision lists may involve multiple cues, as in the second rule in the example ("male and adult"). All decision trees, including fast-and-frugal trees, can be represented as a decision list. And every decision list can be represented as a tree, although not necessarily a fast-and-frugal one. The decision list in the example is not a fast-and-frugal tree, but it makes predictions identical to those of the two trees in figure 4.2.

Constructing a decision list encompasses many more degrees of freedom than constructing a fast-and-frugal tree. It enables combining cues in one rule (such as "male and adult") but also using the same cue repeatedly with different thresholds (such as "over twenty years old"; "over thirty years old"), just as in CART. This freedom leads to large numbers of possible decision lists, and the search for the best-fitting one can become quickly intractable. For this reason, analysts have developed approaches to construct decision lists, such as RIPPER.[49]

Decision trees and decision lists often do not predict as accurately as some other machine learning methods, such as random forests.[50] However, some researchers continue to use them because they view them as transparent.[51] Although these methods are indeed more transparent than, say, random forests, they are generally less transparent than fast-and-frugal trees. Both decision trees and decision lists can become quite complex and difficult to memorize.

4.6   Tallying and Machine Learning

The Keys to the White House apply tallying to predict the next president of the United States. Tallying is a special case of a linear model in which all cues are binary and the weights are +1 or −1. If the tally is above a threshold, the instance is assigned to the target class, otherwise to the other class. If cues are not binary, they can be made so, as discussed in chapter 3. For example, we can transform the age of a person into a binary *adult* cue that is 1 for people older than eighteen and 0 otherwise.

In machine learning, tallying is rare. Many instances of it occur in medical decision making, for diagnosis, treatment choice, and mortality prediction. For example, the *TIMI score* estimates the risk of mortality in patients who have unstable angina.[52] It contains seven cues, including whether the patient is older than sixty-four years and whether the patient had more than two severe angina episodes in the last twenty-four hours. These cues are all binary and weighted equally to arrive at a tally, which is then transformed into an estimated risk of mortality.

A special type of tallying rule uses numeric cues without making them binary. This is called a *unit-weight model*, where cue values are added up (without weighting) to a score. An example is *Más-o-Menos*.[53] In Spanish, *más o menos* means "plus or minus" and "so and so." The first definition describes how tallying works, and the second reminds us that it is designed to work well in the wild rather than be "optimal" in the training data.

Más-o-Menos was used to predict patients' health status out of population, based on genomic cues. Specifically, the task was to predict whether bladder, breast, and ovarian cancer patients would still be alive after five years. To do so, Más-o-Menos needs only to estimate the sign of the association between each cue and survival, that is, the direction of the cue.

Más-o-Menos was compared against ridge and lasso regressions, which require substantial computation to calculate cue weights, on data from twenty-seven medical studies. The number of patients ranged from 17 to 710, with a total of 3,833 in all studies, and the number of cues ranged from 2,463 to 9,768. The studies were conducted in different countries, such as the United States, Sweden, Germany, and Israel. For each cancer type, the three algorithms were trained on the population with the most patients and tested on the other populations. This out-of-population prediction is a proper test case for classification in the wild.

The performance metric was the probability that a patient who survived for a shorter time than another patient received a higher risk score. A value of 0.5 indicates random performance; a value of 1 means that the rankings of the patients by survival time and by risk score are identical.

Table 4.2 shows the average performance and the 95 percent confidence interval in the out-of-population predictions for each cancer type. For predicting bladder cancer, Más-o-Menos performed best, although the confidence intervals of Más-o-Menos and ridge regression overlapped. For predicting breast and ovarian cancers, ridge regression performed best,

Table 4.2

Predicting survival of patients with bladder, breast, and ovarian cancer

	Más-o-Menos	Ridge	Lasso
Bladder	0.71 (0.67–0.74)	0.69 (0.65–0.72)	0.63 (0.58–0.67)
Breast	0.72 (0.69–0.76)	0.78 (0.75–0.81)	0.73 (0.69–0.76)
Ovarian	0.59 (0.56–0.61)	0.60 (0.58–0.63)	0.57 (0.54–0.59)

Out-of-population performance of Más-o-Menos (tallying), ridge regression, and lasso regression, where 1 denotes perfect prediction, and 0.5 denotes random performance (see text). The 95 percent confidence is shown in parentheses.

although all three confidence intervals overlapped. It is fair to conclude that tallying, all in all, performed as well as ridge and lasso regressions.

This study is one of the rare machine learning studies in which predictive accuracy is evaluated out of population. It indicates that tallying could also offer a way forward for constructing interpretable, and at the same time accurate, machine learning models.[54]

4.7   Performance

We have given many examples of successful fast-and-frugal trees and tallying rules throughout the book. In this section, we investigate their performance systematically across a broad range of real-world classification problems.

To judge the performance of a classifier, we apply three criteria: transparency, frugality, and predictive accuracy. Recall the definition of transparency from chapter 1:

A rule is transparent to a group of users if they can understand, memorize, teach, and execute it.

Transparency is a relative concept: a rule can be transparent for an expert group but not for others. Simple heuristics support transparency. In contrast, logistic, ridge, and lasso regressions would be far from transparent for most physicians and paramedics, and the workings of a neural network may not be transparent even to its designer. In this study, we use the number of questions a classifier asks as a proxy for its transparency.

The frugality of a classification rule is defined as the number of cues that one needs to look up to classify instances in a task. If a cue is used multiple times, each time is counted separately. Frugality is not the same as the number of cues. For instance, the HIV tree in chapter 1 has three cues, yet its frugality is only slightly greater than 1 because almost all people exit at the first test.

In chapter 2, we explained two types of errors in classification: misses and false alarms. In many prediction problems, one error is more detrimental than the other. Because we do not know the real importance of errors in the wild, we treat misses and false alarms as equally detrimental. As in chapter 3, we do *not* use total classification error as our performance metric. This error is the proportion of all instances that are misclassified, and can be deceiving if one class is much more prevalent than the other. In the *Titanic* example (fig. 4.2), 1,490 of the 2,201 (68 percent) passengers died. If we simplemindedly predicted death for every passenger, we would not miss anyone who died but would end up with a false alarm rate of 100 percent. The total classification error of this procedure would be only 32 percent, which is the percentage of survivors. A better performance metric is the mean of miss rate and false alarm rate, called *balanced error*. The rule that predicts death for every passenger has a balanced error of 50 percent, the mean of the false alarm rate of 100 percent and the miss rate of 0 percent. Balanced error is not contaminated by the extreme prevalence of one class.

In what follows, we test the relative performance of fast-and-frugal trees, tallying, and machine learning algorithms on a large number (64) of real-world classification problems from a variety of sources, such as machine learning repositories and textbooks.[55] To illustrate, we begin with two examples.

Predicting Diabetes

First we look at a population of 768 Pima Indian women near Phoenix, Arizona. Pima Indians older than thirty-five years have a high prevalence of diabetes, estimated to be around 50 percent.[56] The classification task is to predict who will develop diabetes within five years. Available cues are age, number of pregnancies, plasma glucose concentration, blood pressure, insulin level, body mass index, a body fat estimate, and genetic risk measure accounting for diabetes diagnoses in relatives.

To train fast-and-frugal trees and tallying, we use the Best Fit method discussed in chapter 3.[57] To support transparency, we set the maximum number of cues in tallying and fast-and-frugal trees to six. We compare these heuristics to the decision tree CART, the decision list RIPPER, and random forest. All competitors were trained on 70 percent of the instances and tested on the remaining 30 percent. To obtain stable performance estimates, we repeated this out-of-sample procedure one hundred times (data for out-of-population testing were not available).

Every random sample generated a slightly different classification rule. In figure 4.6, we show the rules learned from the complete data set. The random forest consists of five hundred large trees, one of which is shown in the figure.

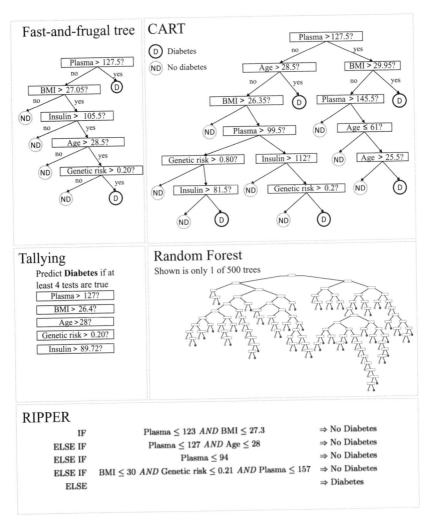

Figure 4.6
Predicting whether a Pima Indian woman will develop diabetes within the next five years. The depicted algorithms are those learned from the entire data set. We do not show a full random forest, but depict only one of its 500 trees.

When predicting diabetes, the balanced error (mean of false alarm and miss rate) of all competitors is very similar (table 4.3). Random forest had the lowest error, but all other methods lagged only one or a few percentage points behind.

Table 4.3

Predicting whether a Pima Indian woman will develop diabetes within the next five years

	Fast-and-frugal tree	Tallying	CART	RIPPER	Random forest
Balanced error	0.28 (0.003)	0.26 (0.003)	0.26 (0.003)	0.27 (0.002)	0.25 (0.002)
Frugality	2.68 (0.04)	5.65 (0.05)	3.14 (0.07)	4.49 (0.19)	Approx. 3,500
Transparency	5.62 (0.05)	5.65 (0.05)	10.60 (0.68)	8.60 (0.52)	Approx. 45,000

We show the mean balanced error, frugality, and transparency for each classifier; in each case, a smaller number is better. For all three measures, standard error is shown in parentheses.

Balanced error is not the only measure of performance. Frugality is the mean number of cues that each algorithm looked up to make classifications. The fast-and-frugal tree is the most frugal rule, closely followed by CART. Random forest is the least frugal. An estimate of its frugality is five hundred times that of an unpruned CART, since trees in a random forest are usually not pruned. A third measure is the total number of questions in a classifier, which we use as a proxy for its transparency.

Predicting Bankruptcy

How can one predict whether a company will go bankrupt? We developed classification rules for predicting which of 9,792 Polish companies would go bust within two years.[58] Sixty-four cues were available, including the profit-to-asset ratio, the gross profit to net sales ratio, and working capital. Of these companies, 515 eventually went bust. The algorithms are the same as in the previous example.

In predicting bankruptcy, CART, RIPPER, and random forest have a balanced error that is two to four percentage points lower than that of the fast-and-frugal tree and tallying (table 4.4). RIPPER slightly outperformed the random forest. The slightly better accuracy of CART and RIPPER comes at the expense of frugality. With 3.11 cues looked up on average, the frugality of the fast-and-frugal tree is by far the lowest among all algorithms, with RIPPER and random forest at the other extreme.

Table 4.4

Predicting whether companies will go bankrupt within two years

	Fast-and-frugal tree	Tallying	CART	RIPPER	Random forest
Balanced error	0.27 (0.002)	0.27 (0.002)	0.25 (0.002)	0.23 (0.002)	0.24 (0.002)
Frugality	3.11 (0.05)	5.93 (0.03)	5.06 (0.08)	27.30 (1.54)	Approx. 4,000
Transparency	5.91 (0.03)	5.93 (0.03)	28.04 (1.16)	85.53 (4.25)	Approx. 125,000

We show the mean balanced error, frugality, and transparency for each classifier; in each case, a smaller number is better. For all three measures, standard error is shown in parentheses.

We do not even try to show a figure with the algorithms corresponding to figure 4.6 because, for instance, each CART contains twenty-eight questions on average. The fast-and-frugal classifiers still ask fewer than six questions on average, while the machine learning algorithms ask substantially more.

The General Picture

Are these two case studies typical of the comparative performance of heuristics and machine learning algorithms? We report the performance of fast-and-frugal trees and tallying compared with CART for sixty-four real-world data sets, including the two examples in the previous sections, containing 95 to 32,561 instances (median 904) and three to 1,418 cues (median 19). These data sets come from medicine, business, law, and the arts, among other fields. As in the examples, the fast-and-frugal trees and tallying were trained with the Best Fit method and limited to using a maximum of six cues.

Each point in figure 4.7 shows the mean balanced error of two algorithms, CART and a heuristic, in one of the sixty-four prediction tasks. The standard error of the mean is shown by a cross. The vertical line in the cross shows two standard errors (on each side of the mean) of CART, and the horizontal line shows the same for the heuristic. First consider the left panel of figure 4.7. If a point is on the diagonal, the balanced error is the same for fast-and-frugal trees and CART; if the point is above the diagonal, the heuristic made more accurate predictions; if the point is below the diagonal,

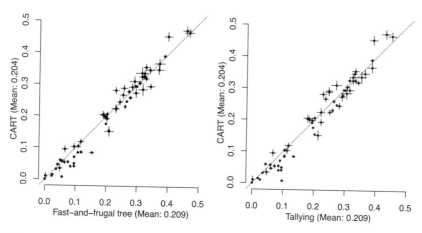

Figure 4.7

Comparison of fast-and-frugal trees and tallying with CART in 64 data sets. Each point shows the mean balanced error in a data set. The vertical and horizontal lines show two standard errors (on each side of the mean) of CART and the fast-and-frugal classifiers.

CART made better predictions. We can see that, across the sixty-four tasks, fast-and-frugal trees predicted nearly as well as CART, falling behind by only half a percentage point on average. We also notice a small advantage for CART in problems where the balanced error is small (balanced error < 0.2), that is, in easy tasks, and a small advantage for fast-and-frugal trees when the balanced error is larger, that is, in more difficult tasks. A similar result emerges when we compare tallying with CART on the same sixty-four tasks (fig. 4.7, right panel).[59]

Although the heuristics and CART show about the same predictive accuracy, their transparency and frugality differ. The mean frugality, which is the mean number of cues looked up, is 5.1 for tallying, 3.8 for CART, and 2.8 for the fast-and-frugal trees. The mean transparency, as measured by the mean number of questions in the tree, is 23.0 for CART, 5.3 for fast-and-frugal trees, and 5.1 for tallying. The average fast-and-frugal tree is considerably simpler and more transparent than the average CART.

Note that these slight differences in performance are measured in out-of-sample prediction. When any of these methods is used in a new context—clinical, financial, or other—the situation is one of out-of-population prediction, and we have no evidence whether these small differences generalize. What we do know, however, is that transparency and frugality generalize.

In summary, we compared the performance of one of machine learning's most transparent algorithms, CART, with fast-and-frugal classifiers. Across sixty-four tests, fast-and-frugal trees predicted about as well as CART but were more frugal and by far more transparent. The same results were obtained for tallying, except with respect to frugality. Thus fast-and-frugal classifiers can substantially increase transparency with little to no loss in accuracy. This outcome demonstrates the transparency-meets-accuracy principle.

4.8   Where Heuristics and Machine Learning Can Meet

Fast-and-frugal classification begins with the question of how humans make decisions. Machine learning begins with the question of how to improve decisions of computers. Nevertheless, these fields are not opposed. As we have seen, fast-and-frugal trees can be translated into decision trees and decision lists from machine learning. Simple heuristics offer the benefit of being more frugal and transparent and can match or exceed the accuracy of more complex algorithms.[60] In many situations, machine learning algorithms perform better than heuristics, most likely in stable worlds—for instance, in games such as chess and Go and in face recognition. On the other hand, simple heuristics can do better in unstable worlds where the future is uncertain and differs from the past in unpredictable ways, such as predicting the spread of the flu or the next president of the United States. The approach of heuristics could offer a way forward for constructing interpretable, and at the same time accurate, machine learning models.

5 Classification in Cognitive Psychology

Without concepts, mental life would be chaotic.
—Edward L. Smith and Douglas L. Medin

When children separate peas from carrots on their dinner plate, they are making a classification. When toddlers say "doggie" when pointing to a dog and "kitty" when pointing to a cat, they are classifying animals. Classification is a fundamental ability that enables higher-level cognitive abilities such as abstraction, thought, and decision making. But how does a toddler know that an animal is a dog as opposed to a cat? What cues do children use? Do they rely on the shape of the eyes, the contour of the head, or the rest of the body? Studies indicate that infants at three months already respond differently to dogs and cats and rely on facial features as well as the contour of the head; bodily features do not seem to play much of a role.[1] Yet researchers do not know precisely which features of faces and heads serve as cues and how they are integrated into a classification rule.

In psychology, classification is mostly called categorization. Much of psychological research addresses the question of how children and adults *form* categories, such as animate versus inanimate, how these relate to language, and whether people prefer a "basic" level of taxonomy that emerges earlier in development, such as *dog* as opposed to *rottweiler* and *animal*.[2] Leaving behind the question of how categories themselves are formed—which, as we explain in chapter 1, is not the subject of the book—this chapter deals with the question of how people assign objects to *existing* categories. How children learn to do so differs substantially from machine learning algorithms. Machines may need thousands of exemplars to reliably classify animals into classes, whereas a child may need to see only a few exemplars.[3]

The cues and classification rules that people use are mostly unconscious. Therefore, conducting interviews with children or adults to uncover these rules does not give us an adequate methodology by itself. People intuitively know which class an object belongs to, but they cannot always articulate *how* they know. Face recognition has the same intuitive quality. Humans excel at recognizing faces, but when asked, many cannot recall the recognized person's eye color or nose shape. For that reason, cognitive psychologists rely on observation of behavior and on experiments to unravel the nature of classification.

5.1 What Is Cognitive Psychology?

Machine learning, the subject of chapter 4, is a prescriptive enterprise. It develops tools such as decision trees and random forests that *should* be used for making accurate classifications. Cognitive psychology, in contrast, is a predominantly descriptive science, whose goal is to discover the processes that underlie human perception, classification, memory, and reasoning. The two disciplines can inform each other: Studying the cues that humans use to assign an object to a class can provide inspiration for the design of robust algorithms. In turn, statistical methods for evaluating the predictive accuracy of models, such as *cross-validation* (i.e., a family of sampling regimes for assessing out-of-sample predictive accuracy), can be used to test theories, such as fast-and-frugal trees, of how people make classifications.

The term *cognition* refers to the mental processes that transform sensory input into behavior. These processes include classification and entail storing, recovering, and integrating information. Cognitive processes have been studied since the beginnings of experimental psychology in the nineteenth century, with a brief interruption in the United States during the first half of the twentieth century, a period in which behaviorism reigned. Behaviorism investigated the relation between sensory input and output, such as the learning of habits and skills, without looking into the "black box" of cognitive processes. It banned mental terms such as *consciousness* and *thought* or anything else that was not directly observable. The "cognitive revolution" of the 1960s eventually overthrew behaviorism, reestablishing the study of mental concepts.

This revolution transformed the very meaning of the nature of cognitive processes. Inspired by the new statistical methods and computers that began to populate psychological labs in the 1950s and 1960s, a new language emerged that pictured cognition as computation, including statistical computation. It may come as a surprise that concepts such as computation and statistical inference were virtually absent in theories of cognitive processes before the cognitive revolution.[4] The analogy between cognition and computation changed how psychologists thought about the nature of cognition and what questions they asked, eventually shaping a new understanding of the nature of categorization. Here is one illustration.

Cognition as Intuitive Statistics

Consider an experiment in which two tones are played in quick succession and listeners are asked whether the tones differ in pitch. If the difference between the tones is smaller than 1 hertz (or 3 Hz for sine waves), then people tend to perceive the tones as identical, otherwise as dissimilar. Since the nineteenth century, psychologists have explained this phenomenon by a "differential threshold"; that is, the two stimuli need to differ by more than a "just noticeable difference" (JND). These JNDs were considered to constitute the elements of the mind; the psychologist Edward Titchener counted some 44,000 of them.[5] In the wake of the cognitive revolution, however, psychologists began to explain the same phenomenon in a fundamentally different way: like a statistician, the mind makes an inference about whether the two tones are the same. Specifically, according to signal detection theory (see chap. 3), the mind calculates two sampling distributions, H_0 and H_1, and a decision criterion.[6] H_0 and H_1 stand for two hypotheses, such as equal or different, signal or noise, disease or no disease. The assumption is that the mind sets a decision criterion to balance the costs of the two possible errors, false alarms (e.g., mistaking two identical tones as different) and misses (e.g., mistaking two different tones as identical). Finally, depending on which side of the criterion the sensory input (tone) falls, the decision is to classify it as identical or different.

In signal detection theory, the problem of classifying two stimuli as the same or different is treated as a statistical decision problem. Signal detection theory was inspired by Neyman and Pearson's statistical decision theory and is formally identical to it.[7] Not only did signal detection theory provide a new way to think about what is going on inside the "black box," but it posed new research questions that had never been asked before. Examples are the questions of how the mind sets the decision criterion and what factors influence the trade-off between the two possible errors.

As mentioned earlier, the idea of cognition as intuitive statistics was virtually absent in psychology before the 1950s. It emerged only after statistical inference became institutionalized in textbooks and curricula as the sine qua non of scientific method beginning in that decade, enabled by the spread of computers. This origin of theories in new scientific tools is an instance of a more general principle of scientific discovery called the *tools-to-theories* heuristic.[8] In sum, the cognitive revolution was more than a revival of the mental and an overthrow of behaviorism: in fact, it changed the very meaning of the mental. Here is where the true revolution occurred.

As we will see, the program of the mind as an intuitive statistician became highly influential in psychological research on classification.

5.2   Two Cultures in Studying Classification

In the early stages of the cognitive revolution, classification was studied with artificial objects designed by experimenters, such as triangles and circles or line drawings of faces and planes that varied in terms of two to four attributes.[9] Classes were defined by necessary and sufficient conditions, such as geometrical objects that are small, white, and round. Under the influence of Egon Brunswik's probabilistic perspective, the logical relation between features and classes was extended to probabilistic relations, such as that the feature *white* indicates a category in 90 percent as opposed to 100 percent of the cases.[10] However, unlike in Brunswik's ecological program, which studied the cue-class correlations in the natural environment, the objects, classes, and probabilities were now typically determined by the experimenter. Beginning in the 1970s and 1980s, researchers proposed complex statistical models to describe how humans make classifications, using similar artificial objects and classes in experiments. We will refer to this culture in which the experimenter designs artificial objects and the classification rule as classification *in the lab* (see chap. 1).

In contrast to the categories in the lab culture, most, if not all, "natural" categories cannot be defined logically, as the psychologist Eleanor Rosch has emphasized. *Natural* here means that these categories are part of the natural experience of humans, such as dogs, trees, friends, and foes.[11]

Unlike artificial categories, natural categories tend to have ill-defined boundaries. In addition, their members are not equally representative, although there are prototypes or, precisely speaking, members that are more or less "prototypical." Preschool children can identify a sparrow, but not as easily an ostrich or penguin, as a bird.[12] Similarly, adults may perceive a German shepherd as a more prototypical dog than a wire-haired dachshund, though it is difficult to define logically what a dog is—after all, a dog with three legs or without hair is still a dog. Natural categories present a challenge to the study of artificial categories defined by logical or probabilistic rules: one cannot know whether the processes people rely on to classify artificial objects are similar to those they use for classifying natural objects.

The alternative is to study directly how people classify natural objects rather than artificial ones. We refer to this culture as the psychological study of classification *in the wild*. It has its origins in Rosch's work, but also in Herbert Simon's writings on bounded rationality.[13] Simon argued that under uncertainty, which, as discussed in chapter 1, is a defining feature of the wild, people have to *satisfice* rather than optimize. Satisficing means finding a good solution when the optimal solution cannot be known. In these situations, people rely on fast-and-frugal heuristics and other psychological tools. The important difference between this and the lab culture is that the experimenter does not start with a known classification rule defined on the basis of artificial objects. Rather, the goal is to discover the rules people actually use to make classification in the wild, which could be tallying, fast-and-frugal trees, or something else.

The existence of multiple classification rules is captured in the concept of the *adaptive toolbox* in analogy to a physical toolbox, where one needs particular tools to solve different tasks, such as a hammer to drive a nail into a board.[14] It is called "adaptive" to highlight a functional perspective, which is useful to understand cognition, keeping in mind that brains evolved to solve problems of survival and reproduction. Applied to classification, this concept requires the rules to be fast and frugal, that is, to work quickly with limited information instead of relying on exhaustive information searches and time-consuming algorithms that border on intractability.

For instance, to distinguish friend from foe at a distance, face recognition should function even when the visual image is still blurred. However, humans need proximity and proper light for inspecting the eyes, nose, mouth, and other internal features of a face. Accordingly, studies indicate that humans rely on the external shape of the head, which is easier to recognize at a distance, and on the relationship of this shape to the internal facial features.[15] Classification at a distance also requires tolerance for degradation and incomplete information. Highly degraded pictures, such as a photo of Albert Einstein with a pixel count of 19 × 25, will be unrecognizable close-up but can be reliably identified at a distance.[16]

We have distinguished two cultures in the psychological study of classification. In classification in the lab, the experimenter designs artificial objects and a classification rule and then uses this framework to study people's behavior. In classification in the wild, the researcher selects natural objects for which the classification rule is not known, and then studies how people assign objects to natural classes.

5.3   Classification in the Wild

In psychology, the study of heuristics goes back to the Gestalt psychologists in the first half of the twentieth century. The heuristics they considered were general and informal, such as information search by "looking around." Formal models of heuristics were not introduced until after the cognitive revolution, by mathematical psychologists such as Amos Tversky. In the following years, a large number of studies demonstrated that people use heuristics for making decisions, for instance, about what to buy and where to invest, among others.[17] Similarly, behavioral biologists studied the rules of thumb that animals use for choosing nest sites, food sites, and mates.[18] In psychological research on classification, however, models of heuristics are fairly new.

Classification by Counting and Ordering

Heuristics are based on core cognitive capacities that include ordering and counting. Counting is an ability that children develop early in life. It entails assigning to every object in a set an ordered sequence of number terms, such as one, two, three. It is based on the principles of correspondence (one-to-one mapping of object and number term) and succession.[19] By the time children are two years old, most have developed a stable counting sequence but need another year or so to realize that the cardinal number of the set is the final count. Given a picture with three birds, young children may count "one, two, three" without grasping that the final tally represents the total number of birds. Tallying is also the principle that the first civilized humans used to represent numbers: a tally of fingers or notches on a stick, or writing "four" as "IIII" in Egyptian hieroglyphic notation.[20]

The tallying heuristic is based on counting; it treats all cues as equally important. In situations where cues vary in their importance, ordering can replace counting. A particularly useful principle is lexicographic ordering, embedded in fast-and-frugal trees, as we saw in chapter 3. As explained there, this process is named "lexicographic" on account of how people look up a word in a lexicon, starting with its first letter, then the second, and so on. One of the most important inventions in mathematics is the lexicographic number system known as the Arabic system, invented by mathematicians in India in the first centuries AD. Unlike the earlier number systems, including the Roman version, this positional system has a strict order, with a zero as placeholder. To find out which of two numbers is larger, one looks at their first digit, and if these differ, the larger digit indicates the larger number; none of the other digits need to be inspected. If the first digit does not differ, then one continues with the second digit, and so on. This principle is implemented in fast-and-frugal trees.

As we will see in chapter 6, lexicographic ordering can also promote safety. Consider traffic rules about the right-of-way. Cues are set in a fixed order: first, the hand signal of the police officer regulating traffic; second, the color of the traffic light; third, the traffic sign; and fourth, the direction from which another car is coming (left or right). The first cue dominates the second, and so on. None of the cues are weighted or integrated, which would inevitably lead to chaos.

Psychological Research on Tallying

Some of the earliest uses of tallying in psychology appear in intelligence testing. Here the problem lies in deciding how to weight the responses to the many questions in an IQ test. The common practice has been to weight them equally and simply count the number of correct answers.

Tallying rules are also found in the allocation of scarce resources in uncertain situations. For instance, studies report that venture capitalists rely on tallying when they select business plans or predict whether a venture will be financially successful.[21] Allocating money equally to N assets is a well-known investment heuristic:

1/N heuristic: Invest your money equally to N assets.

Despite often being ridiculed as naive, this simple tallying heuristic can perform as well as or better than the Nobel Prize–winning mean-variance portfolio and other fancy investment strategies.[22] Many parents rely on $1/N$ to allocate the scarce resources of time and attention to their children, where N is the number of children in the family. The $1/N$ heuristic achieves its purpose in two-child families but leads to the paradoxical result that, in families with three or more children, the middle children end up with less total time from their parents during their youth in comparison to their oldest and youngest siblings.[23] Equal sharing is likewise a principle of democratic voting systems where every vote has the same weight. It is also part of the "wisdom of the crowds," where the (unweighted) average of people's estimates can lead to excellent predictions. The classical demonstration of this idea goes back to Francis Galton, cousin of Charles Darwin, who found, much to his surprise, that the average of people's estimates of the weight of an ox at a county fair was very close to its true weight.

Tallying also plays a role in social situations where people decide how to react to others' behavior. In a study on forgiveness, participants were asked to recall an incident in which they had felt wronged, let down, betrayed, or hurt by a friend, romantic partner, or colleague.[24] The authors found that the following heuristic predicted (not just fitted) about 70 percent of decisions whether or not to forgive the wrongdoer:

Forgiveness heuristic: Forgive unless the wrongdoer intended to do harm and is to blame and did not apologize sincerely.

People using this heuristic rely on three questions: Intended to harm? Is to blame? Apologized sincerely? Only if all three answers are "yes" is the wrongdoer not forgiven. In other words, if the tally is three affirmatives, do not forgive; otherwise forgive.

Like the bail-or-jail tree in chapter 1, the forgiveness heuristic can be represented both as tallying and as a fast-and-frugal tree. The fast-and-frugal tree comprises the three questions, the first two solely with the exit "forgive" if the answer is "no," and the final question with both the exits "forgive" and "not forgive." As explained in chapter 3, a fast-and-frugal tree can be represented by tallying if all its exits, except for those of the last cue, lead to the same classification. In these cases, the order of cues does not matter for the action taken, only for the process in which cues are looked up, which can be relevant to speed and frugality.

Yet how accurate are predictions based on a simple tally compared to the estimation of regression weights? The psychologist Robin Dawes conducted one of the first studies on this question.[25] He investigated how well faculty ratings of graduate students' performance ("outstanding," "very good," and so on) could be predicted from students' GRE scores, their GPA, and a measure of the selectivity of the students' undergraduate institution. Using cross-validation, a linear multiple regression achieved a correlation of 0.38. Yet when Dawes replaced the "optimal" regression weight with random weights (numbers between 0 and 1), the correlation increased to 0.48. For other prediction problems, he found similar results and concluded: "The whole trick is to know what variables to look at and then know how to add."[26] To simplify the procedure even further, researchers such as Hillel Einhorn and Robin Hogarth replaced random weights with unit weights (i.e., tallying, all weights equal to 1) and found similar results.[27] They argued that one should always test regression models against tallying and that one needs to test for prediction, not data fitting. Mere data fitting, however, was at that time the norm in psychology, as it was in the *Journal of the American Statistical Association*.[28]

Dawes provided the random weights with the correct signs. Jean Czerlinski and colleagues went on to show that even when tallying (with equal weights) has to estimate the signs—the cue directions, as they were called in chapters 2 and 3—from learning samples, its predictive accuracy (cross-validation) was on average slightly better than that of linear multiple regression across twenty studies (fig. 5.1).[29] Even better was the predictive accuracy of a lexicographic heuristic similar to fast-and-frugal trees (*take-the-best*),[30] which is also shown in figure 5.1. The amount of overfitting in all three strategies can be inferred from the decline between fitting and prediction. Tallying overfits when the signs of the cues are estimated with error.

More than three decades after the discovery of the predictive power of tallying, Hogarth reviewed the literature to see how well this result had penetrated psychology and economics.[31] An analysis of five standard textbooks in econometrics revealed no mention of tallying and its performance. The

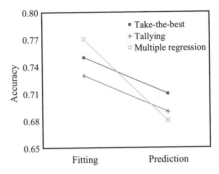

Figure 5.1
Less is more: fitting and out-of-sample predictive accuracy of tallying and take-the-best (a lexicographic heuristic similar to a fast-and-frugal tree) in twenty real-world tasks, taken from economics, business, biology, and other fields. The accuracy of ordinary linear multiple regression is also shown as a benchmark. See text for details.

major exceptions are psychometric textbooks that emphasize using equal weights. Hogarth concluded that the predictive power of tallying is not entirely ignored in psychology but is poorly understood and has had little influence on the widespread use of regression analysis to model human behavior. In his view, researchers find it hard to accept that simple heuristics can solve complex problems, although there is still hope that this insight will eventually survive in the marketplace of ideas.

In medical diagnosis and treatment choice, tallying appears to be used relatively more frequently. Beyond Más-o-Menos, which we discussed in chapter 4, other examples include the Kocher Criteria for Septic Arthritis,[32] which estimate the risk of septic arthritis for children with an inflamed hip; the TIMI score,[33] which estimates the risk of mortality for patients with unstable angina; the Quick SOFA score,[34] which predicts mortality in patients with suspected infection; the HAS-BLED score,[35] which estimates the risk of major bleeding for patients on anticoagulation medication; the AWOL score,[36] which predicts the risk of delirium during hospitalization; and the CURB-65 score,[37] which estimates mortality for individuals with community-acquired pneumonia.

All in all, tallying remains a largely unexplored process in psychology, as it is in machine learning. Its potential use for classification has barely been considered.

Psychological Research on Fast-and-Frugal Trees

Fast-and-frugal trees are members of a class of heuristics that search through cues in an order and stop searching when a cue allows making a decision. As mentioned earlier, they belong to a larger class known as lexicographic heuristics, which have been studied mostly outside of classification, such as for choices between two or more alternatives (as in fig. 5.1). Examples include take-the-best and Amos Tversky's *elimination-by-aspects*.[38]

Few empirical studies exist on elimination-by-aspects, but take-the-best has been tested in a large number of experiments. The general conclusion is that in conditions where it is ecologically rational, take-the-best can predict choices, reaction times, and other behavior for a substantial proportion of people.[39] At the same time, the heuristic shows an excellent predictive accuracy (fig. 5.1). Such results have been since replicated and extended.[40] Demonstrations that simple heuristics can be both descriptive *and* highly accurate contradict the widespread view that people's use of heuristics is problematic or even irrational.[41] But in the wild, simplicity can indeed be better.[42]

Psychological studies of classification have only recently considered fast-and-frugal trees. This omission is surprising, given that practitioners have long been using fast-and-frugal trees (chap. 1). The first study we know of examined allocating patients with severe chest pain to either the intensive care unit or a regular bed (chap. 2). The physicians who conducted the study were inspired by a talk given by one of this book's authors (GG) on take-the-best, and they adapted the heuristic to the classification of patients. Since then, several studies have documented and tested the use of fast-and-frugal trees in health care, when investigating both how physicians actually make classifications and how they should make them.

Medical studies using fast-and-frugal trees include descriptive investigations of how general practitioners decide whether or not to prescribe antidepressants to patients,[43] how they decide whether or not to prescribe lipid-lowering drugs,[44] and how they diagnose hyperlipidemia and heart failure.[45] A prescriptive study designed fast-and-frugal trees for classifying children with community-acquired pneumonia as needing or not needing macrolide prescription to counteract the undesirable development that many children have become macrolide resistant.[46] Other prescriptive studies designed and tested fast-and-frugal trees for detecting depression,[47] for using statins for primary prevention of cardiovascular diseases,[48] for differentiating asymptomatic bacteriuria from catheter-associated urinary tract infections,[49] and for guiding practitioners through end-of-life care decisions for patients with dementia.[50] Using information technology and a genotype database, a general fast-and-frugal tree methodology has been developed to translate pharmacogenomics data to aid in medication selection, thereby supporting personalized medicine.[51]

Several empirical studies have also been conducted outside the clinical domain. A study on personnel decisions concluded that nearly half of college students and more than two-thirds of experienced managers relied on fast-and-frugal trees to decide which employee gets a bonus and which should be fired.[52] Prescriptive analysis concluded that fast-and-frugal trees would provide efficient guidelines for mobile apps when users need to make choices out of a set of alternatives offered by the app,[53] and that if drivers followed a fast-and-frugal tree for deciding which parking space to take, parking congestion would be relieved.[54]

In summary, a number of studies have investigated tallying and fast-and-frugal trees as descriptive or prescriptive models of classification in the wild. Yet, as we will see in the next section, these heuristics are virtually absent in traditional experimental research on categorization in the lab. This tradition mostly limits itself to the question of how artificial stimuli are assigned to artificial classes.

5.4   Classification in the Lab

The view that cognition is statistical inference became particularly influential in research on classification, where various statistical theories turned into theories of how the mind allocates objects to classes. As explained earlier, the mind-as-statistician view had a direct impact on what kind of classification tasks researchers studied. Consider the objects in a typical study (fig. 5.2).[55] The geometrical figures have been constructed by varying four attributes: shape, size, color, and location.

Participants sit in front of a computer screen (represented by the rectangles in fig. 5.2) and need to learn that the *small white triangles* that appear on the *left side* of the screen belong to a class labeled *A*, whereas the *large black circles* that appear on the *right side* of the screen belong to a class labeled *B*.

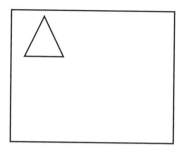
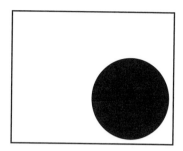

Figure 5.2

A typical psychological classification experiment in the lab. Participants have to learn to assign stimuli such as small white triangles on the left of a computer screen to one class and large black circles on the right of a computer screen to another class.

People quickly learn to make these kinds of classifications perfectly, and thus the research has focused on issues such as the time course of classification and its speed. It often takes less than one second to make a classification in the lab. Theorists have gone to great lengths to model what transpires in participants' minds in that tiny amount of time. To do so, statistical algorithms have been assumed, adjusted, and extended, reaching considerable sophistication. To review this literature here would be a daunting task.[56]

In the next sections, we therefore do not aim at providing a sweeping overview but instead describe briefly some key ideas of this program and how it differs from classification in the wild. We focus on what are called *exemplar-based random walk* models. Like Bayesian models, these estimate the probabilities that objects belong to particular classes.[57] Note that we do not explicitly discuss Bayesian models, because they involve computations of probabilities that can easily become intractable.[58]

Exemplar-Based Random Walks

The key idea of exemplar-based theories is that an object, once encountered, is stored in memory as a point in a k-dimensional space, where k is the number of cues on which the objects vary (such as the four cues in fig. 5.2).[59] Exemplar-based theories have been combined with random walks and Abraham Wald's sequential decision theory.[60] Wald's theory in turn is a sequential version of Neyman and Pearson's statistical decision theory, which, as mentioned, inspired signal detection theory. We describe here the basics of the *exemplar-based* random walk model of classification in simplified form to aid exposition.[61]

To illustrate, we use the ischemic heart disease problem introduced in chapter 2. Consider a physician who has to classify a new patient, Mark, as belonging to one of two classes: low (C_0) or high (C_1) risk of ischemic heart disease. The doctor makes the classification on the basis of the patient's values on $k = 3$ binary cues, which are whether the ST segment in the electrocardiogram is elevated, whether chest pain is the chief complaint, and whether other symptoms, such as history of heart disease, are present. As in chapters 2 and 3, a patient's cue profile—also called a symptom profile—is denoted by a string showing the patient's cue values. That is, if Mark has an elevated ST segment (1), chest pain is his main complaint (1), and no other symptoms are present (0), then his profile is 110.

Exemplars

In the heart disease problem, exemplars are previous patients whose cue values and classes have been stored in a physician's memory. To make it simple, assume that information is stored for three exemplars (the number of stored exemplars would be much larger for an experienced physician). Patients 101 and 011 belong to the high-risk class C_1 after having had a subsequent heart attack, whereas patient 010 belongs to the low-risk class C_0 because no heart attack subsequently occurred.

According to the exemplar-based random walk model, at a series of moments in time, the physician will retrieve one of the previous patients' information from memory. This retrieval is determined by the symptom profile of the new patient Mark in the following way.

Encountering Mark, the physician has some probability of retrieving information for each previous patient. This probability is a function of the similarity between each previous patient and Mark. In the simplest case, the similarity is measured by the number of cues on which the two patients have the same value. Given that Mark's symptom profile is 110, patients 101 and 011 each have a similarity of 1 to Mark, whereas patient 010 has a similarity of 2. The probability of retrieving a particular patient is the ratio of this patient's similarity to Mark over the sum of all similarities of all previous patients stored in memory to Mark. In our situation, the retrieval probabilities are ¼ for 101, ¼ for 011, and ½ for 010.

The assumption is that the physician keeps two counters, one for high risk and one for low risk. Both counters start at 0. Once a patient is retrieved, one of two counters is increased. If the retrieved patient had a heart disease, the high-risk counter is increased by 1; otherwise the low-risk counter is increased by 1. The same patient can be retrieved more than once. As soon as one counter reaches a predetermined threshold, such as 2, the physician will assign Mark to the corresponding class. This process is represented in figure 5.3.

For example, when the physician encounters Mark, whose symptom profile is 110, there is a ½ probability that the patient with symptom profile 010 will be retrieved from the physician's memory. This patient has been assigned to the low-risk class C_0, and thus the counter N_0 in favor of class C_0 for Mark will be set to 1. The counter N_1 will remain equal to 0. Because no counter has yet reached the threshold of 2, another memory retrieval will take place. If the next patient retrieved from the physician's memory has symptom profile 101, which is an event occurring with probability ¼, N_1 will be set to 1, and one more retrieval from memory will be necessary. Assuming that this is again the patient with symptom profile 010, N_0 will

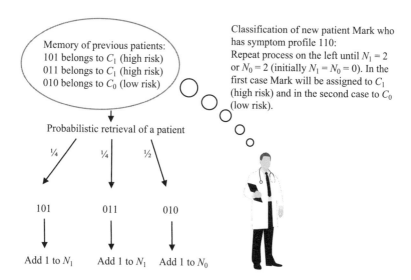

Figure 5.3
A representation of a simple version of the exemplar-based random walk model. The counter N_0 records evidence in favor of low-risk class C_0 for the new patient Mark. Similarly, the counter N_1 records evidence in favor of high-risk class C_1.

be set to 2, and the process will be terminated, with Mark being assigned to the low-risk class C_0.

The actual models in the psychological literature are far more complicated. For instance, the storage of exemplars in memory can be subject to encoding errors; the computation of similarity between exemplars could be made sensitive to the varied importance of cues; the retrieval of information from memory might use different subsets of cues at different moments in time; the counters recording evidence in favor of classes could initially be set to unequal values, as could the thresholds required for deciding on each class; and so forth. Furthermore, some models have used additional concepts such as mental architecture, which denotes whether information is processed serially or in parallel and whether search is always exhaustive or may terminate via the application of a stopping rule.[62] Such extensions have been implemented by using up to a dozen free parameters.[63]

To the best of our knowledge, exemplar-based random walk models have not been tested in the wild. In principle, they could be tested for the classification problems we have looked at in previous chapters, such as whether to bail or jail a potential criminal. At the same time, in the wild, the ideal assumptions of the exemplar model are unlikely to hold. For instance, physicians would need access to exemplars, including feedback, which presents a problem. Like magistrates, physicians in most health systems do not have access to the data to represent the people they are classifying in a k-dimensional space, for one because they do not have complete feedback on whether patients they diagnosed with a disease actually had it. Patients often do not return, and medical systems do not always keep complete statistics or keep them in an easily accessible form. An additional complication is that too many cues may be available, as we saw in Dhami's bail-or-jail study in chapter 1, which featured twenty-five cues. Theories such as exemplar models provide no basis for deciding which of those cues people focus on.

5.5 Research Strategy in the Wild and in the Lab

Cognitive Processes

Unlike curve-fitting models, cognitive models are derived from basic principles of cognition.[64] For example, although Brunswik used linear regression, he did not think that it describes cognitive processes, viewing it instead as a convenient data-modeling procedure. One reason is that regression makes assumptions such as normality and homogeneity that are often inconsistent with what we know about cognition, such as response times that are not symmetric and whose variance increases with the mean. In random walks, the future state depends on the last state alone, not on its history. The same "memoryless" principle—that memory past the last state does not matter—is now assumed as a property of the mind. This principle, however, does not generally describe how physicians and other experts make classifications.[65] In general, using statistical tools as models of the mind requires a critical look at their assumptions.

The exemplar component of exemplar-based random walks has also been criticized for its intractability and consequently for its psychological implausibility: potentially, a prohibitively large number of exemplars would need to be stored in memory.[66] In fact, this criticism motivated the development of simpler versions that assume that a new object is compared not with all stored objects but only with a prototype (often defined as the mean) or, even more simply, with its nearest neighbor.[67]

On the basis of this analysis, it appears unclear to what degree exemplar-based random walk models are valid process models. Yet articles in psychology and beyond routinely refer to them as process models. They have their origins in statistical tools and were subsequently reconsidered as models of the mind. This is another case of the tools-to-theories heuristic in science and, more specifically, in the psychology of classification.[68]

Fitting or Prediction?

Exemplar models may include a dozen free parameters for memory encoding, measures of similarity, information retrieval, and rules for stopping information search in a stochastic way. This approach provides high flexibility in data fitting but is not necessarily an advantage, because flexibility can decrease the accuracy of predictions. Fast-and-frugal trees and tallying, in contrast, are less flexible. As we saw in preceding chapters and will see again in chapter 6, fast-and-frugal trees and tallying have been used for predicting in the wild. For instance, the bail-or-jail tree has been tested using cross-validation to predict the behavior of magistrates out of sample, while the thirteen Keys to the White House constitute an example of out-of-population prediction.

Have exemplar-based random walk models been tested in predicting human behavior? Until the 1990s, one would have had to search hard to find any predictions in cognitive modeling in general. The philosopher of science Clark Glymour's phrase "We can model that" bitingly summarizes the data-fitting-oriented mind-set that, with a sufficient number of adjustable parameters, everything can be modeled after the fact.[69] In the 2000s, psychologists began increasingly to recognize the importance of prediction.[70]

This lesson does not appear to have been heeded in classification in the lab. Some applications of model-selection procedures do exist, such as the Bayesian information criterion and also cross-validation. But on the whole, the systematic application of these methods is missing in classification in the lab. Furthermore, we could not find any instances of out-of-population prediction in the lab.

Flexibility

Flexible models of classification fit data better but may not predict well (recall the gerrymandering illustration in chap. 4). The fewer behaviors a rule excludes, the more flexible it is, and the harder it is to falsify it. At one extreme, a flexible rule can explain every single behavior after the fact. That is, no behavior is excluded by such rules, and they cannot be refuted. An exemplar-based random walk with a dozen free parameters can fit a large range of behaviors, and it is not always clear which behavior is inconsistent with the theory. At the other extreme, an inflexible rule predicts just one or a small range of behaviors and excludes many others. An example is the $1/N$ rule for allocation, which implies one, and only one, allocation of assets while being inconsistent with everything else.

Classification rules with little or no flexibility can make *strong* predictions. A strong prediction is one that is unlikely to be true unless a particular theory holds. Strong predictions are useful because, unlike weak predictions, if they are accurate, they will lead to large knowledge gains.[71] The same point holds for classification. Rule-based models such as fast-and-frugal trees are less flexible, more parsimonious, and bolder in the sense of Karl Popper than stochastic models with many free parameters.[72]

Table 5.1 summarizes the typical differences in research strategy between classification in the lab (e.g., exemplar-based random walks) and classification in the wild (fast-and-frugal trees and tallying).

Table 5.1

Typical differences in research strategy between classification in the lab and in the wild

	Classification in the lab	Classification in the wild
Objects	Artificial objects designed by experimenters, such as triangles and circles that vary on 2 or 3 cues	Natural objects, such as patients suspected of heart disease, that vary on an unknown number of cues
Classes	Artificial classes defined by experimenters, such as category A and B	Natural classes, such as heart disease that occurs in the natural environment
Cognitive process	Exemplar-based random walks can make implausible demands on memory, and to what degree they are compatible with the known facts of cognitive processing remains unclear.	Heuristics describe a sequence of cognitive operations, based on counting or ordering, that can be tested.
Fitting or prediction?	Focus on fitting parameters to known data observed in the past. Little or no use of cross-validation or other generalization criteria. No attempts at out-of-population prediction.	Focus on predicting behaviors in the future. Systematic use of cross-validation, similar to machine learning. Some out-of-population prediction.
Flexibility	Exemplar-based random walks typically have a large number of free parameters and can fit data well after the fact. This flexibility can lead to weak predictions (i.e., predictions that are likely to be true based on all or most available theories).	Heuristics use zero or a small number of free parameters. This limited flexibility reduces the ability to fit data after the fact and can lead to strong predictions (i.e., predictions that are unlikely to be true unless a particular theory holds).

The differences listed in table 5.1 are not exhaustive. For instance, fast-and-frugal trees and tallying can make only ordinal predictions about classification speed, whereas exemplar-based random walk models make quantitative predictions. The heuristics have provided transparent practical guidelines for action, as in the paramedic tree and HIV tree; exemplar-based random walk models have not. Thus a future research direction is to investigate how we can use these two approaches to inform each other, in the spirit of a toolbox of simple heuristics and other more complex strategies.[73]

5.6   The Complexity Paradox

The most elementary form of classification is enumeration, where a category is essentially the set of its members ("my family"). No classification rule is needed. When children are exposed to small numbers of novel items from an unfamiliar category, they do exactly that by remembering individual exemplars.[74] With more exemplars, however, enumeration no longer works, and one needs classification rules based on cues. Classification is in essence uncertain inference.

Psychological research has developed two programs to study how people make such inferences. Classification in the lab studies how people classify artificial objects that have been designed to vary on few attributes in situations where the classification rule is defined by the experimenter. Classification in the wild studies how people classify natural objects that vary on an unknown number of attributes, and the classification rule is yet to be discovered.

Our analysis of these two approaches leads to a seemingly paradoxical conclusion. Research on classification in the lab has proposed complex statistical models to describe how people solve easy tasks. Research on classification in the wild has shown that simple heuristics describe how people solve difficult tasks.

6 Building a Safer World

The safety of the people shall be the highest law.
—Cicero

On January 15, 2009, US Airways Flight 1549 departed from LaGuardia Airport in New York City, its destination Seattle-Tacoma International Airport. Within two minutes after takeoff, a flock of Canada geese collided with the plane's two engines and improbably disabled both of them. Captain Sullenberger and copilot Skiles had to make a difficult decision: could the plane make it all the way back to LaGuardia, or to another airport, or would they have to attempt an emergency landing in the Hudson River?

Sullenberger and Skiles could have tried to measure speed, wind, altitude, and distance to estimate whether the plane could reach the LaGuardia runway. Yet how accurate would that estimate be? And did they have sufficient time to make these calculations? Both captain and copilot knew that they had barely enough time to go through the dual-engine failure checklist, let alone to make complex calculations. Instead Sullenberger and Skiles resorted to a simple rule of thumb. In the copilot's words: "It's not so much a mathematical calculation as visual, in that when you are flying in an airplane, things that—a point that you can't reach will actually rise in your windshield. A point that you are going to overfly will descend in your windshield."[1] The rule of thumb is the following:

Gaze heuristic: Fix your gaze on the control tower. If the tower rises in the windshield, the plane cannot reach the runway.

This fast-and-frugal heuristic not only requires just a single piece of information but is also immune to errors of calculation. Because the LaGuardia tower rose in their windshield, Sullenberger and Skiles decided to land in the Hudson River. As multiple simulations have shown afterward, they made the correct decision. The pilots managed to land the plane without any casualties.

The version of the gaze heuristic just described is adapted to safety in landing, but the heuristic applies to solving coordination problems in general. Versions of the same heuristic are used, among others, by sailors to avoid collisions with other boats, by baseball outfielders to catch a ball, by dogs to catch a Frisbee, and by hawks to intercept doves.[2]

People have a widespread belief that complex problems need complex solutions.[3] But the "miracle on the Hudson" illustrates how a simple classification rule can save lives. After investigating the accuracy, frugality, and transparency of fast-and-frugal classification rules in the previous chapters, we now investigate how they can increase safety. We examine fast-and-frugal trees in two challenging situations where safety is a priority: identifying a suicide attacker at a military checkpoint and identifying banks on the brink of collapse. In both cases, we describe how a fast-and-frugal tree was constructed through the *practitioner method*. This is a process for designing simple rules not by using statistical methods alone, as described in chapters 2, 3, and 4, but by consulting with experts, as well.

6.1   Friend or Foe?

In areas troubled by war or other serious conflicts, peacekeeping operations aim to create a stable environment. Such operations include ground patrols, military convoys, and checkpoints. Figure 6.1 portrays a NATO checkpoint in Afghanistan.

A crucial task for soldiers manning checkpoints is to classify oncoming traffic as friendly or hostile. This classification can make the difference between life and death for the soldiers as well as for the occupants of an approaching vehicle. If soldiers infer that a vehicle contains civilians, they will use warning signals to make it slow down and eventually stop so that it can be searched and approved for further travel. If the soldiers infer that the vehicle may be occupied by suicide attackers, they will escalate the use of force to eliminate the threat.

This process is fraught with uncertainty. Civilians frequently drive so close to convoys or checkpoints that they appear to be threats.[4] They might

Figure 6.1

A NATO checkpoint manned by British soldiers in Helmand province, Afghanistan.
Used with permission of Reuters Images.

do so because they are nervous, or because they cannot understand the
soldiers' requests.[5] Additionally, people working for the government might
suspect a checkpoint to be one of the bogus checkpoints that insurgents
sometimes set up to arrest or kill government officials. The consequences of
this uncertainty can be dire. In 2006, the Multi-National Corps–Iraq began
compiling statistics on checkpoint encounters. In January and February
2006, more than six hundred incidents were recorded in which civilians
had appeared to be a threat. Civilians were injured in more than sixty of
these incidents and killed in more than thirty. Between 2003 and early
2006, an estimated number of more than one thousand Iraqi civilians were
killed at checkpoints.[6]

NATO, national armies, local authorities, activist groups, and the public
mutually agree that decreasing the number of civilian casualties is a moral
imperative. It is also strategically important for peacekeeping because civilian deaths increase local resentment, which can in turn lead to new suicide
attacks. The military has reacted to this situation by issuing directives for
the disciplined use of force.[7] These directives have been successful in situations when use of force can be approved though a chain of command.[8] But

that is not the situation confronting soldiers who have to assess a potential threat on their own and within seconds. In such cases, no reductions of civilian casualties have been reported. A solution to this lasting problem would be a classification rule for reliably distinguishing civilians from attackers. This rule should be transparent and fast so that soldiers can memorize and quickly apply it.

Before we show how such a classification rule can be developed, let us take a closer look at the actual situation of the soldiers.

NATO Rules Are of Little Help

For engaging with oncoming traffic, NATO commanders and soldiers are commonly provided with rules listed on cards.[9] One such card, prepared for the Kosovo War in 1999, is shown in figure 6.2. Rule 3 of this figure prescribes the *escalation of force*:

a. Shout verbal warnings.

b. Show a weapon, which would be ready to use.

c. Use the weapon, if necessary.

d. Use non-lethal force, such as targeting the vehicle to neutralize it.

e. Employ force, possibly lethal, such as shooting, to destroy the vehicle and kill or neutralize its occupants.

Note that this card does not supply any classification rules for distinguishing civilians from suicide attackers. Nor does it give any guidance about when soldiers should increase the level of force, retain the current level, or stop applying force and simply walk up to the vehicle to initiate the search. Instead it makes vague statements such as "When the situation permits, use a graduated escalation of force."

How, then, do soldiers distinguish civilians from suicide attackers? We do not know. But we can analyze official reports of encounters between soldiers and incoming vehicles to get clues. We describe these 1,053 reports in detail in the next sections. The main insight from this analysis is that soldiers appear to rely essentially on a single cue: whether the oncoming vehicle is *complying* (i.e., slowing down or stopping) or not.[10] Compliance was the only cue mentioned in all the 1,053 reports involving civilians. In 1,020 of these cases, soldiers escalated force as soon as the vehicle failed to comply. Conversely, as long as the vehicle complied, force was not increased. Thus the soldiers' behavior can largely be summarized by the following rule.

PEACE ENFORCEMENT: KFOR (Albania, April 1999)

TASK FORCE HAWK ROE CARD
(The contents of this card are unclassified for dissemination to Soldiers)

NOTHING IN THESE RULES PROHIBITS OUR FORCES FROM EXERCISING THEIR INHERENT RIGHT OF SELF DEFENSE.

1. AT ALL TIMES, USE NECESSARY FORCE, UP TO AND INCLUDING DEADLY FORCE:
   a. In response to an immediate threat of serious bodily injury or death against yourself, other NATO Forces, or the Friendly Forces of other nations.
   b. To prevent the immediate theft, damage, or destruction of: firearms, ammunition, explosives or property designated as vital to national security.

2. AT ALL TIMES, USE FORCE LESS THAN DEADLY FORCE:
   a. In response to a threat less than serious bodily injury or death against yourself, other NATO Forces, or the Friendly Forces of other nations.
   b. To prevent the immediate theft, damage, or destruction of any NATO military property.

3. WHEN THE SITUATION PERMITS, USE A GRADUATED ESCALATION OF FORCE, TO INCLUDE:
   a. Verbal warnings to "Halt" or "ndalOHnee"
   b. Show your weapons.
   c. Show of force to include riot control formations.
   d. Non-lethal physical force.
   e. If necessary to stop an immediate threat of serious bodily harm or death, engage the threat with deliberately aimed shots until it is no longer a threat.

4. SOLDIERS MAY SEARCH, DISARM, AND DETAIN PERSONS AS REQUIRED TO PROTECT THE FORCE. DETAINEES WILL BE TURNED OVER TO APPROPRIATE HOST NATION AUTHORITIES ASAP.

5. WARNING SHOTS ARE STRICTLY PROHIBITED.

6. TREAT ALL EPWs WITH DIGNITY AND RESPECT. RESPECT THE CULTURAL AND RELIGIOUS BELIEFS OF ALL EPWs.

7. DO NOT RETAIN WAR TROPHIES OR ENEMY SOUVENIRS FOR YOUR PERSONAL USE.

8. DO NOT ENTER ANY MOSQUE, OR OTHER ISLAMIC RELIGIOUS SITE UNLESS NECESSARY FOR MISSION ACCOMPLISHMENT AND DIRECTED BY YOUR COMMANDER.

9. IMMEDIATELY REPORT ANY VIOLATIONS OF THE LAW OF WAR, OR THE RULES OF ENGAGEMENT TO YOUR CHAIN OF COMMAND, MPs, CHAPLAIN, IG, OR JAG OFFICER REGARDLESS OF WHETHER FRIENDLY FORCES OR ENEMY FORCES COMMITTED THE SUSPECTED VIOLATION.

10. THE AMOUNT OF FORCE AND TYPE OF WEAPONS USED SHOULD NOT SURPASS THAT AMOUNT CONSIDERED NECESSARY FOR MISSION ACCOMPLISHMENT. MINIMIZE ANY COLLATERAL DAMAGE.

Figure 6.2
A card given to NATO commanders and soldiers involved in peacekeeping in the operation Kosovo Force (KFOR) in Albania in April 1999, prescribing the rules of engagement (ROE) with oncoming traffic.

Compliance heuristic: Increase the level of force only if the oncoming vehicle is not complying.

Soldiers increased force, as in level (c), in 857 of the 1,053 incidents. These shots led to thirty-five civilian casualties. In the other 196 of the 1,053 incidents, soldiers employed the highest force levels of shooting at the vehicle or the people, as in levels (d) or (e), resulting in another 169 casualties. Note that increasing force from as in level (c) to as in (d) did not make the vehicle comply. Increasing force to (e), by definition, did. In sum, soldiers overescalated the use of force, apparently due to using an overly simple heuristic that relies on just one cue, and caused too many civilian casualties. Is there a less harmful strategy?

A Fast-and-Frugal Tree for Identifying Suicide Attackers

To solve the problem of civilian casualties, the psychologist Niklas Keller and one of us (KK) developed a classification rule for identifying suicide attackers that can be applied quickly in the wild.[11] We did this in three steps.

Step 1: *Identify cues.*

Cues need to have two properties: they need to be (1) highly predictive and (2) easy and fast to observe. To find such cues, we first scanned the literature, including military documents. For example, the presence of more than one occupant in a vehicle has been mentioned as a "valuable indicator" of civilian status.[12] In 2006, Lieutenant General Peter Chiarelli, the second highest ranking US general in Iraq at that time, stated in an interview with *Stars and Stripes* that he wanted soldiers to "count heads" in a vehicle.[13] This approach is intuitive: suicide attackers are high-value assets from the attackers' perspective, so assigning multiple attackers to a single vehicle would be a waste of resources. After reviewing the literature, we conducted semistructured interviews with armed forces instructors and combat-experienced personnel. Interviewees were asked to comment on cues mentioned by other interviewees or in the literature. This process yielded three cues: *multiple occupants*, *compliance*, and *further threat cues*. An example of a threat cue is an intelligence report about a suspicious blue Honda Civic in the area.

Step 2: *Identify a heuristic.*

Using the cues identified in step 1, we then need to ask which type of heuristic would be more appropriate for the problem at hand. Specifically, the heuristic should be easy to memorize, quick to apply, and accurate in its predictions. In a fast-and-frugal tree, cues are ordered in importance, whereas in tallying, they have equal weight. Both types of heuristics are easy to memorize. However, the tree allows personnel to make classifications faster than does tallying because they can make a decision after the first or second cue, without having to use all three cues. In addition, one of the three cues, multiple occupants, is likely to be a very strong one. This argues for ordering the cues rather than weighting them equally and counting. Thus both requirements, deciding quickly and accurately, point toward using a fast-and-frugal tree.

Step 3: *Build the heuristic.*

Constructing a fast-and-frugal tree requires identifying reasons and ordering them. All interviewed practitioners—military personnel of the German Army—indicated that a vehicle with multiple occupants is a strong indicator of civilian rather than suicide attacker status. They also believed that noncompliance is a strong indicator of a suicide attacker, but indicated that the first reason was much stronger than the second. In addition, checking for multiple occupants first makes the application of the tree potentially highly efficient in areas with much carpooling (because of low vehicle density, as in Afghanistan). Practitioners commented that such a speedy rule would be an effective stress reliever for soldiers. The second reason in the fast-and-frugal tree is noncompliance, intuitively used in soldiers' "compliance heuristic." This correspondence with existing practice could contribute to how easily soldiers understand, accept, and apply the fast-and-frugal tree.

Figure 6.3 shows the final *Checkpoint Tree*. It can be printed on a pocket card, disseminated to soldiers, and easily memorized. The first question is whether the vehicle contains more than one occupant. If so, then the inference is that they are nonhostile civilians. Otherwise a second question is asked, whether the vehicle is not complying. If so, the classification is that the vehicle occupant is hostile. Otherwise a third question finally classifies all remaining vehicles. The Checkpoint Tree is transparent and frugal. But how accurate is it?

A Test of the Checkpoint Tree

Empirical data for evaluating the Checkpoint Tree are hard to come by. After the tree was constructed, however, a political scandal made relevant data available. In 2010, WikiLeaks made public 91,000 documents from the war in Afghanistan, most of which were classified as secret. Among the

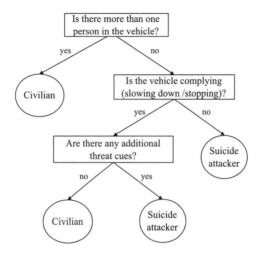

Figure 6.3
The Checkpoint Tree: a fast-and-frugal tree for identifying an oncoming vehicle as
containing suicide attackers or civilians, constructed using the practitioner method.

leaked data were 1,060 official reports from Afghanistan checkpoints that
recorded critical (i.e., not routine) encounters between soldiers and oncoming vehicles from 2004 to 2009.[14] Here is an example of the relevant part of
a report, where sensitive information is replaced by "X," and explanations
of abbreviations are provided in parentheses.

> At XXXX TF (task force) Kandahar reports XXXXXXXXXXXXXXXX
> section injured 2x LN's (local nationals) at XXXXXXX in XXXXXX
> district of XXXXX province. A white Toyota corolla with 2x LN's in
> it was approaching too fast, FF (friendly forces) told vehicle to stop a
> number of times, vehicle failed to stop. FF engaged vehicle wounding
> 1x LN in car and 2nd LN (child) ran into mosque wounded.

As one can see from the example, the reports allow identifying the outcome of the encounter—whether civilian or military casualties occurred,
and if so, how many—and the values of cues, such as whether the vehicle
slowed down or stopped and the number of occupants in the vehicle. Among
the 1,060 reported incidents, seven were suicide attacks, and in each of
these, the vehicle contained exactly one suicide attacker. NATO forces were
not able to stop the attacks in these seven cases, which all succeeded. For

understandable reasons, no other information is available about these particular incidents. In the remaining 1,053 incidents, the vehicles approaching the checkpoints included civilians only. Soldiers incorrectly classified
some of these civilians as suicide bombers. Consequently, 58 civilians were
killed, and another 146 were injured.

For the seven cases of successful suicide attacks, we do not have enough
information to test the Checkpoint Tree. We know that they always involved
a single occupant, but we do not know whether the driver complied or
whether soldiers were influenced by additional intelligence information.
What we can say with certainty is that because all the attacks succeeded,
the Checkpoint Tree could not have performed any worse than the soldiers.

For the remaining 1,053 cases, which all entailed civilians, the reports
provide enough information to test the tree. In these cases, it correctly classified 975 as involving civilians and incorrectly classified 78 as involving
suicide attackers. How would these 78 false alarms translate into a number
of civilian casualties?

Assume that soldiers have memorized the Checkpoint Tree and now
apply it. Classifying someone as a suicide attacker does not imply that the
person will be killed or even injured. As the escalation-of-force rules show,
shooting at people or vehicles occurs only at the highest two levels. According to the "battle damage assessment" reports, the soldiers indeed reacted
in a nuanced way. Thus we can reasonably assume that a number of these
78 individuals would not have been harmed even if flagged as a threat. A
study of the reports on these cases reveals only 13 casualties (5 killed and
8 injured) among them. But it is difficult to know what the exact number
of casualties would have been had the soldiers used the Checkpoint Tree.
We can, however, take 78 as an upper limit. Compared with the 204 actual
casualties caused by the soldiers, this would amount to a reduction of at
least 60 percent of civilian casualties, and probably many more.

How Was the Checkpoint Tree Received?

The German Army Command has highlighted the Checkpoint Tree in its
classified training-and-lessons-learned monthly newsletter *Aus dem Ein-
satz lernen* (Learning from deployment). The Command evaluated the
study as applicable to a wide range of situations in which military action
includes deciding whether to escalate force. Additionally, the Command
recommended the Checkpoint Tree as a tool for team leaders and mission

instructors. We believe that NATO and other forces involved in peacekeeping operations should use the Checkpoint Tree as a systematic decision aid that is highly accurate and easily applicable.

After *Science News* published a report titled "Decision Tree for Soldiers Could Reduce Civilian Deaths," a reader expressed concern that suicide attackers would try to "game" the tree.[15] For example, attackers could start carpooling to be classified as civilians at the first level of the tree. This is a reasonable concern. There are also reasonable responses to it.

First, at the time of writing this book—more than four years after the *Science News* report was published—we know of no such carpooling. Furthermore, carpooling would automatically multiply suicide attackers' lives lost without increasing the damage they inflict. One might argue that suicide attackers could use a mannequin to give the impression of a second occupant. To guard against this possible scenario, soldiers can be trained to recognize such attempts, perhaps by using high-quality infrared visual aids.

In the next section, we present a second case study of classification in the wild that also aims at using simple rules for improving safety.

6.2   The Dog and the Frisbee

On August 31, 2012, in Jackson Hole, Wyoming, Andrew Haldane—then executive director of financial stability at the Bank of England and later the bank's chief economist—gave a speech titled "The Dog and the Frisbee" at the Economic Policy Symposium of the Federal Reserve Bank of Kansas City.[16] Although dogs and Frisbees appear an unlikely contribution to economic policy, just hours after the speech, the *Wall Street Journal* commented in a blog that "people . . . and markets . . . should long remember" Haldane's words and later hailed it as the speech of the year.[17] Why?

Haldane's speech echoed the theme of this book: how to use simple rules to solve complex problems. Dogs catch flying Frisbees much in the same way as experienced baseball players catch fly balls—by adjusting their speed so that the angle of gaze to the Frisbee or ball remains constant. This is the same heuristic used in the Hudson River landing. Haldane compared it to financial regulation:

> Catching a crisis, like catching a Frisbee, is difficult. Doing so requires the regulator to weigh a complex array of financial and psychological factors, among them innovation and risk appetite. . . . Yet despite this complexity, efforts to catch the

crisis have continued to escalate. . . . So what is the secret of the watchdog's failure? The answer is simple. Or rather, it is complexity. For what this paper explores is why the type of complex regulation developed over recent decades might not just be costly and cumbersome but sub-optimal for crisis control. In financial regulation, less may be more.[18]

Haldane pointed out that financial institutions and regulators are missing something important. They have been employing the standard models of finance theory, which rely on known probability distributions, without asking enough questions about the applicability of such models. By and large, the mathematical models used today by bankers, financial economists, and regulators rely on an extremely large number of parameters that need to be estimated under uncertainty and are not developed with an eye toward increasing transparency. One might thus suspect that they likely do not work as well in the wild. Value-at-risk models purport to safely estimate the capital a bank needs to avoid bankruptcy with a high enough "probability," such as 99.9 percent. Yet they did not stop 42 of 116 big global banks (i.e., banks with more than US$100 billion each in assets at the end of 2006) from failing during the financial crisis that followed.[19] David Viniar, then chief financial officer of the investment bank Goldman Sachs, could not believe his eyes when he saw twenty-five-sigma events occur several days in a row, resulting in huge losses for the company.[20] According to such risk models, a five-sigma event is expected to occur once between now and the last Ice Age ten thousand years ago, and an eight-sigma event only once between now and the Big Bang; a twenty-five-sigma event is beyond human imagination. The problem is not bad luck but rather models that are not fit to deal with uncertainty.

Blaming the modelers is too easy. Taking a more holistic view, one can observe a predominant trend of building overly complex and opaque financial systems matched by overly complex and opaque financial regulatory frameworks.[21] But it does not have to be this way. In fact, it has not always been this way. To better understand the ever-increasing complexity of the regulatory framework, let us count the number of pages in the three versions of the most famous international financial regulatory framework, the Basel Accords: Basel I (1988) was a modest 30 pages, Basel II (2004) 347 pages, and Basel III (2010) 616 pages.

What do the Basel Accords regulate? Relevant here are the parts on how to determine the capital requirements of a bank. In Basel I, the regulations were extremely simple, focused on a limited set of credit risks, and applied to all banks. Gradually, however, Basel I was perceived as lacking sensitivity to risk. In Basel II, banks could use their own internal models, which allowed for increasingly larger risks, tailored to each bank's exposure. As such, the models became more mathematically flexible. This move toward complexity continued for almost three decades. On the basis of Basel III, a large bank needs to estimate thousands of risk values. Because these risks correlate, the number of parameters that need to be estimated is likely to be in the millions.

As Mervyn King, former governor of the Bank of England, famously said, if banks were playing in a casino—and it is often said they do—one could estimate these parameters. But banks operate in the wild. Among other factors, new opaque financial products, whose consequences nobody can anticipate, increase uncertainty. Some analysts suspect that applying financial models designed for a world of known risks to the wild was one of the causes of the 2008 financial crisis. The economist Joseph Stiglitz noted after the crisis: "It simply wasn't true that a world with almost perfect information was very similar to one in which there was perfect information."[22]

Attempting to cope with risk, the Basel Accords created more uncertainty by introducing more complex regulation. At the same time, transparency has also taken a blow from regulators allowing each bank to use its own internal models and estimate its own millions of parameters.

Moreover, as analyzed in Haldane's Jackson Hole speech, the complexity of the Basel Accords has intensified demands on the financial industry. In 2013, banks in the United Kingdom were required to fill in more than 7,500 cells of data to provide the required information to financial regulators. A midsize European bank would thereby need two hundred new full-time positions, according to a study by McKinsey & Company.[23] Correspondingly, the number of financial regulators in the United Kingdom has also risen almost fortyfold, from one regulator required for every 11,000 people working in the financial sector in 1980 to one regulator required for every 300 three decades later. Government and industry need to invest in a staggering number of new jobs merely to keep up with the Basel framework.

Reactions to Haldane's speech were mixed. An editorial in the *Guardian* titled "Finance and Risk: On Knowing Too Much" commented hopefully that "financial economics is heading back to the world as Keynes and Hayek knew it: where economic uncertainty was recognized as such, rather than mathematized and mis-sold as controllable risks."[24] But it is not at all clear whether economics is anywhere close to abandoning unnecessarily complex models. In his comment on the speech while at Jackson Hole, Erkki Liikanen, former governor of the Bank of Finland, cited the saying that for every complex problem there is an answer that is clear, simple, and wrong. Liikanen is but one in the huge choir of voices that continue to equate simplicity with error.

Can regulators and bankers discard some of the current complexity and opacity without sacrificing accuracy? Little work has addressed this question. Here we examine whether it is possible to identify failing banks in advance by using simple and transparent models.

How to Identify Failing Banks?

Central banks appoint experts such as financial economists to supervise commercial banks. A crucial task of supervisors is to classify banks as being at a "high" risk of failure or not. Banks identified as high-risk should be monitored more closely, and central banks intervene to avoid having clients lose their savings and employees lose their salaries.

One tool traditionally employed by financial heavyweights such as the International Monetary Fund to estimate the risk that a bank might fail is logistic regression. The results of regressions are used in conversations among policy makers, including politicians and members of a central bank's financial stability committee. These results are also communicated to the public.

This practice has two issues. First, it is not easy to know how satisfactory the accuracy achieved by regression is, because it is typically not compared with the accuracy of alternative models. Thus how much confidence one should place in the results of regression remains unclear. Second, many recipients of the information might lack a background in economics or econometrics. To them, a regression is not transparent; they cannot understand it and are thus reluctant to rely on it. Like medical doctors, the majority of policy makers and politicians might require simpler and more transparent models than logistic regression.

A team of economists from the Bank of England plus two of this book's authors (GG and KK) addressed both of these issues.[25] They gathered data on 116 global banks with more than US$100 billion in assets at the end of 2006 (see also chap. 3). This period is often considered the beginning of the financial crisis. Eleven economic cues, such as leverage ratio and wholesale funding level, were gathered for each bank.

Data sources included the balance sheets of banks, official reports, and publicly available reports from stock markets. In some cases, cross-checks necessitated the revision of data. Data gathering lasted many months. After the crisis, it was known which of the banks failed and which did not.

In what follows, we explain how to construct a fast-and-frugal tree for predicting bank failure, after which we compare its predictive accuracy with that of a more complex way of combining these cues, namely, logistic regression.

A Fast-and-Frugal Tree for Identifying Failing Banks

This section describes the steps used to construct a fast-and-frugal tree for identifying failing banks by using the practitioner method. The steps are essentially the same as the ones used to construct the fast-and-frugal tree for identifying suicide attackers (the Checkpoint Tree) but have been adapted to reflect the different characteristics of the bank failure problem and special requests made by the decision makers. A technical difference is that the practitioners—economists at the Bank of England—relied on some *exploratory data analyses*.[26] That is, here the art of classification was combined with science. Unlike inferential statistics, this kind of statistics does not attempt to compute probabilities of hypotheses or optimize estimators. Rather, it attempts to provide insight into the data by inspecting simple measures of central tendency or dispersion, as well as graphics.

Step 1: *Identify cues.*

Initially, the team of practitioners, led by Sujit Kapadia, an economist for the Bank of England, identified eleven cues as potentially useful for predicting bank failure. For each cue, the team examined how well it distinguished between banks that did and did not fail. The team then selected a small number of cues: *leverage ratio, market-based capital ratio,* and *loan-to-deposit ratio.* Leverage ratio is the ratio of a bank's Tier 1 capital (capital from, e.g., common stock and disclosed reserves) to its total assets. Total assets are calculated as in tallying, without using risk weights. Market-based capital ratio is the ratio of a bank's market capitalization (the market value of the bank's outstanding shares) to its total assets, where total assets are now calculated by using risk weights. The third cue, loan-to-deposit ratio, applies to the bank's retail customers. This cue was preferred to cues with comparable correlation to bank failure, such as wholesale funding ratio, because the latter were not easy to record accurately.

Step 2: *Identify a heuristic.*

The practitioners suggested using a fast-and-frugal tree as a decision aid for regulators that would make transparent the logic of what might cause banks to fail. This transparency was said to support conversation among stakeholders, especially those without a strong background in economics, econometrics, or other quantitative disciplines.

Step 3: *Build the heuristic.*

The leverage ratio cue was placed first because it distinguished best between banks that failed and those that did not fail. The economists from the Bank of England argued that the case of a bank having a small leverage ratio should lead to an exit and classification of the bank as being at a high risk of failing because it does not have enough capital. The value of the threshold of leverage ratio that best discriminated between banks that failed and those that did not fail was fitted to be 4.1.[27] On the basis of expert opinion, the team placed market-based capital ratio as the second cue. The fitted value of this cue's threshold was 16.8. In line with the logic regarding the leverage ratio, a market-based capital ratio with a value of less than 16.8 led to an exit and classification of the bank as being at high risk. Finally, the third cue was retail loan-to-deposit ratio, with a fitted threshold value of 1.4. The tree is shown in figure 6.4.

Consider the Swiss Bank UBS, which required substantial support from the Swiss authorities to survive the crisis. At the end of 2006, the bank had a leverage ratio of 1.7 percent, which would have resulted in a red flag. In contrast, it had a market-based capital ratio and a loan-to-deposit ratio that satisfied the other thresholds. In a regression model, a low leverage ratio can always be compensated by sufficiently good values on the other cues. A fast-and-frugal tree, in contrast, is noncompensatory; that is, no such trade-offs are possible. This logic is akin to the functioning of complex human bodies: a failing heart cannot be compensated by perfect lungs and kidneys.

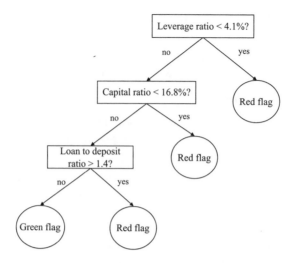

Figure 6.4
A fast-and-frugal tree for identifying a bank at a high risk of failing or not, constructed using the practitioner method.

Note that the fast-and-frugal tree of figure 6.4 can also be represented as a tallying heuristic. The reason is that every question has a "red flag" exit. A bank receives a green flag if and only if all three cues are negative. The practitioners found the graphical tree representation easier to understand and more practicable.

Regressions and Trees: How Accurately Can They Identify Failing Banks?

The economist David Aikman and his colleagues compared the practitioners' fast-and-frugal tree in figure 6.4 with logistic regressions and statistically induced fast-and-frugal trees.[28] The study excluded banks in the dataset that had missing cue values, leaving 74 banks, of which 29 eventually failed and 45 did not.

The statistically induced fast-and-frugal trees were calibrated by cross-validation with a training set consisting of 70 percent of banks over one thousand repetitions. There were twenty such trees with varying cue orders and exit structures. Each corresponded to a different value of a parameter w, which expressed the relative weight of false alarms and hits and was used to determine the order of cues and the prediction of each cue as follows:

The *loss* of a cue equaled w Pr[false alarm] – $(1-w)$ Pr[hit], where $w = 0.05$, $0.1, \ldots, 0.95$. For each w, cues were ordered in increasing order of their loss, and the predictions in the nodes (green versus red flag) were chosen so as to minimize the loss of the whole tree. Twenty regressions were calibrated in the same way as the statistically induced fast-and-frugal trees. The only difference was that each regression included an additional parameter t that translated the output of the regression, a probability p of bank failure, into a binary judgment as follows: if $p > t$, then the bank is at a high risk of failing; otherwise it is not.

The tree in figure 6.4 achieved a hit rate of 86 percent and a false alarm rate of 53 percent. In other words, this fast-and-frugal tree correctly classified 25 of the 29 banks that eventually failed as being at a high risk of failing, and incorrectly classified 24 of the 45 banks that did not fail as being at a high risk of failing. None of the logistic regressions could simultaneously achieve a hit rate *and* a false alarm rate that were better than those of the fast-and-frugal tree. For example, if any regression correctly classified more than 25 of the 29 failed banks, it incorrectly classified more than 24 of the 45 failed banks. The same holds for the statistically induced fast-and-frugal trees. That is, no statistically induced model dominates the tree constructed by the practitioner method.

Figure 6.5 depicts the performances of the three approaches. The cross represents the fast-and-frugal tree constructed using the practitioner method (fig. 6.4), the squares represent statistical fast-and-frugal trees, and the circles represent logistic regressions. No point is located to the left of and above the practitioner tree.

As can be seen in figure 6.5, the predictive accuracy of the regressions and the statistically induced trees is similar for small hit and false alarm rates, while for higher values, the fast-and-frugal trees consistently result in higher accuracy. The area under the curve equals 0.75 for the statistically induced fast-and-frugal trees and 0.72 for the logistic regressions. The transparency-meets-accuracy principle is at work here.

Fast-and-Frugal Regulation

In the preceding section, we demonstrated that fast-and-frugal trees can predict as well as or even better than standard economic tools such as logistic regression. Yet the thresholds of the tree in figure 6.4 were estimated for a specific population of banks at a specific period in time. Because banks

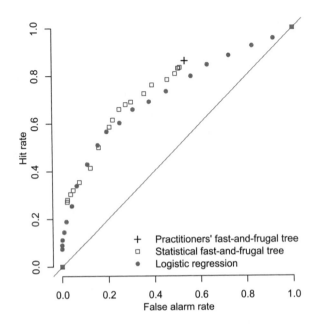

Figure 6.5
The predictive accuracy of the fast-and-frugal tree constructed using the practitioner method (fig. 6.4), compared with logistic regressions and statistically induced fast-and-frugal trees.

operate in the wild, it is unlikely that these thresholds would apply to other populations and other times. To turn the predictive tree into a regulatory tree, one needs to add a safety factor to the thresholds. This is akin to a civil engineer calculating the safety characteristics of a bridge and then doubling them for the actual construction of the bridge.

Our collaborating practitioners have suggested a threshold of 10 percent for the leverage ratio and a threshold of 20 percent for the market-based capital ratio. A 10 percent leverage ratio would introduce a large safety margin and has also been suggested by Mervyn King. In the foregoing data set, this safety margin would have red-flagged all big global banks examined at the beginning of the 2008 financial crisis. Implementing such a margin would not only allow banks to scrap most of the documentation required by Basel III but also make stress tests obsolete. Although such large safety margins would likely meet with resistance from banks—who profit from having low capital—there is a good point to be made that safeguarding the public should take priority over the financial interests of investment bankers.[29]

Bank lobbyists who resist simple and transparent regulation argue that simple rules can easily be gamed by banks. It is true that simple rules can be gamed, as can every regulation. But in fact the existing complex rules have already been gamed by banks: their increasing complexity makes it even easier to find loopholes and twist the millions of risk estimates. All of this has led to unproductive activities, such as an adverse race in complexity between bankers and regulators. Unlike complex regulation, gaming of simple rules is easier to detect and counter.

6.3   Simplicity Can Enable Safety

Checkpoint decision making and bank regulation are examples of trying to keep safe in the wild. Here complex situations require sufficiently simple rules, not overly complex ones. For the soldiers, the fast-and-frugal tree provides a systematic guideline for action. The tree is easy to teach and memorize and can be followed quickly in situations of danger. It can reduce casualties caused by soldiers by 60 percent or possibly more and thus save many civilians' lives. The case of banking regulation differs in that a regulatory framework is already in place. The framework is overly complex, however, and allows banks to use internal models to estimate thousands of risk factors and millions of correlations to calculate their value at risk, which determines their capital requirement. Given this complexity, it is hardly possible for regulators to evaluate the correctness of these estimates, and banks have incentives to twist the estimates so that they need to own as little capital as possible. Despite their failure to prevent the financial crisis of 2008, regulators and politicians alike nevertheless continue to uphold the belief that complex situations require complex solutions. As we have seen, however, the method of fine-tuning and optimizing does not work well in the wild; instead it makes systems fragile and provides illusions of certainty.

Fast-and-frugal trees are not the only simple rules that can enable safety in the highly interconnected world of finance. Consider the rule "Don't buy financial products you don't understand."[30] If everyone on both sides of the Atlantic had followed this rule before the crisis, it would not have happened to the same extent. The rule refers to derivatives and other complex financial instruments, which already in 2003 the investor Warren

Buffett called "weapons of mass destruction." Another helpful rule comes from the former trader Nassim Taleb: "Trust only people who have skin in the game."[31] In investment, this means entrusting your money to bankers who have their own money invested, as in family-owned banks. Family-owned banks plan for the next generation, not the next quarterly report, and have little incentive to make short-term profit at the cost of risking long-term loss. Under uncertainty, simple rules can provide safety where complex regulation fails.

7 Conclusions

I can live with uncertainty and not knowing. I think it's much more interesting to live not knowing than to have answers which might be wrong.

—Richard Feynman

We wrote this book against the prevailing belief that complex methods of classification are always better and more data always lead to more accuracy. Although this belief is true in situations of certainty and complete control, where the future resembles the past, it does not necessarily hold in situations of uncertainty and lack of control. In such situations, simple rules can predict more accurately on the basis of less information and are more transparent and understandable to boot. We have used the terms *in the lab* and *in the wild* as a shorthand for these situations; many real-life situations have elements of both.

A key proposition is that *simple rules do well in the wild*. This is the *unstable-world principle*, which states that if the future differs from the past in unpredictable ways, then keep it simple. As we have seen, doing well has multiple meanings. First, the process of classification should be transparent; that is, users should be able to understand, memorize, teach, and execute it. For a long time, both machine learning and cognitive psychology did not take transparency seriously. Researchers focused instead on accuracy. Finding highly complex models that fitted or predicted an iota better was believed to be the goal of science, assuming that these fine-tuned solutions would actually be robust when situations change. This attitude is now being called into question in the move toward understandable AI and through European residents' right to explainable algorithms, as stated in the General

Data Protection Regulation. Citizens have begun to demand the right to understand why an algorithm classified them as not worthy of a loan, a job, higher education, or parole. Transparency is a key value in itself.

Furthermore, transparency and accuracy are not mutually exclusive but can in fact be compatible. Under uncertainty, simple and transparent rules tend to improve accuracy, which we call the *transparency-meets-accuracy principle*. One reason why a degree of simplicity can increase predictive accuracy is illustrated by the bias-variance dilemma. Yet this insight is not yet generally appreciated, particularly when research communities simply fit classification rules to data without putting them to the test of prediction. In data fitting, complexity always wins. Therefore all tests of classification rules need to be performed not by fitting data but by predicting, ideally *out of population*. Furthermore, complex models should be compared to simple rules.

Finally, these ideas exist within a larger societal context. Simple rules can support citizens in becoming more autonomous. This can include simple nutritional rules, such as "don't eat anything your great-grandmother would not recognize as food" and "avoid food products you see advertised on television."[1] Providing people with such rules could help people categorize what they are eating and navigate their way out of the obesity epidemic or not arrive there in the first place. Similarly, simple rules for financial investment could be taught in school, so that people learn at an early age to evaluate the risks and opportunities they face to better manage their money.[2] In general, rules that people can easily memorize and follow can provide them with efficient tools for attaining self-empowerment. Empowering humans is a crucial goal for a philosophy of machine learning that goes beyond merely enhancing algorithms.[3]

Classification in the Wild brings together ideas from machine learning and cognitive psychology. In the digital age, the wild is rapidly becoming a world of algorithms and of increasing complexity. To master this new world, machine learning can learn from psychology and vice versa. The human brain has evolved for dealing with the wild and the uncertainty spawned by nature and other humans. The fast-and-frugal heuristics that the brain uses to tame uncertainty can provide concrete inspirations for machine learning. The key insight we offer is that one can make algorithms simple, understandable, and accurate at the same time.

Notes

Introduction

1. Our title *Classification in the Wild* is reminiscent of the anthropologist Edwin Hutchins's 1995 classic *Cognition in the Wild*, a book full of insights that apply the principal metaphor of cognitive science, cognition as computation, to the structure of work aboard large ships. While we are not in the business of sailing, the book navigates through other parts of the wild, presenting precise algorithms for taming uncertainty.

2. Leonard J. Savage, *The Foundations of Statistics* (Mineola, NY: Dover, 1954).

3. See, e.g., Gary A. Klein, *Sources of Power: How People Make Decisions* (Cambridge, MA: MIT Press, 1998).

4. Cynthia Rudin and Joanna Radin also make this point in "Why Are We Using Black Box Models in AI When We Don't Need To? A Lesson from an Explainable AI Competition," *Harvard Data Science Review* 1, no. 2 (2019).

5. Herbert A. Simon, *Models of Bounded Rationality: Empirically Grounded Economic Reason* (Cambridge, MA: MIT Press, 1997).

6. Gerd Gigerenzer, Peter M. Todd, and the ABC Research Group, *Simple Heuristics That Make Us Smart* (New York: Oxford University Press, 1999); Gerd Gigerenzer, Ralph Hertwig, and Thorsten Pachur, eds., *Heuristics: The Foundations of Adaptive Behavior* (New York: Oxford University Press, 2011); Peter M. Todd, Gerd Gigerenzer, and the ABC Research Group, *Ecological Rationality: Intelligence in the World* (New York: Oxford University Press, 2012); Ralph Hertwig, Ulrich Hoffrage, and the ABC Research Group, *Simple Heuristics in a Social World* (New York: Oxford University Press, 2013); Ralph Hertwig, Timothy J. Pleskac, Thorsten Pachur, and the Center for Adaptive Rationality, *Taming Uncertainty* (Cambridge, MA: MIT Press, 2019).

Chapter 1

1. William K. Estes, *Classification and Cognition* (New York: Oxford University Press, 1994), chap. 5.

2. Note that this is a definition of terms; it is not a statement about all lab studies. One could study classification tasks that are ill-defined in the lab, but this is only rarely done.

3. Josh Katz, "Who Will Be President?" Upshot, *New York Times*, 2016, November 8, 2016, https://www.nytimes.com/interactive/2016/upshot/presidential-polls-forecast .html?_r=0; https://projects.fivethirtyeight.com/2016-election-forecast. Two weeks earlier, Silver's various models had predicted up to a 95 percent chance for Clinton.

4. John Markman, "Big Data and the 2016 Election," *Forbes*, August 8, 2016, https://www.forbes.com/sites/jonmarkman/2016/08/08/big-data-and-the-2016-elec tion/#5e5678e71450.

5. Alan J. Lichtman, *Predicting the Next President: The Keys to the White House* (Lanham, MD: Rowman and Littlefield, 2016).

6. Peter W. Stevenson, "Trump Is Headed for a Win, Says Professor Who Has Predicted 30 Years of Presidential Outcomes Correctly," *Washington Post*, September 23, 2016, https://www.washingtonpost.com/news/the-fix/wp/2016/09/23/trump-is -headed-for-a-win-says-professor-whos-predicted-30-years-of-presidential-outcomes -correctly/?utm_term=.e3a8b731325c.

7. In 44 of the 49 elections since 1824, the winner of the popular vote also won the election. Hillary Clinton won the popular vote by 2.1 percent.

8. Philip E. Converse, "The Nature of Belief Systems in Mass Publics," in *Ideology and Discontent*, ed. David Apter (New York: Free Press, 1964): 206–261.

9. Gerd Gigerenzer, *Gut Feelings: The Intelligence of the Unconscious* (New York: Penguin, 2007), chap. 8.

10. Gerd Gigerenzer, *Calculated Risk: How to Know When Numbers Deceive You.* (New York: Simon & Schuster, 2002), chap. 7.

11. *HIV* here refers to HIV-1, which is the main family of HIV and accounts for about 95 percent of infections worldwide. HIV-2 is endemic to West Africa.

12. Virginia A. Moyer, "Screening for HIV: US Preventive Services Task Force Recommendation Statement," *Annals of Internal Medicine* 159, no. 1 (2013): 51–60.

13. Roman Prinz et al., "What Counselors Tell Low-Risk Clients about HIV Test Performance," *Current HIV Research* 13, no. 5 (2015): 369–380, https://doi.org/10.2174/ 1570162X13666150511125200.

14. Gigerenzer, *Calculated Risk*, chap. 7.

15. Prinz et al., "What Counselors Tell Low-Risk Clients."

16. This result is based on HIV testing in 752 US laboratories; see Roger Chou et al., "Screening for HIV: A Review of the Evidence for the US Preventive Services Task Force," *Annals of Internal Medicine* 143, no. 1 (2005): 55–73.

17. An additional complication of expanding a fast-and-frugal tree is that one would need to specify how to break ties, such as between one positive and one negative ELISA test result.

18. Nora M. Doyle, Judy E. Levinson, and Michael O. Gardner, "Rapid versus Enzyme-Linked Immunosorbent Assay Screening in a Low-Risk Mexican American Population Presenting in Labor: A Cost-Effectiveness Analysis," *American Journal of Obstetrics and Gynecology* 193, no. 5 (2005): 1280–1285.

19. D. Hammond, "The Effects of Remand," *Prison Service Journal*, no. 69 (1988): 19.

20. The Bail Act 1976 and its subsequent revisions; see Mandeep K. Dhami and Peter Ayton, "Bailing and Jailing the Fast and Frugal Way," *Journal of Behavioral Decision Making* 14, no. 2 (2001): 141–168.

21. Dhami and Ayton, "Bailing and Jailing," 163.

22. Mandeep K. Dhami, personal communication, 2003.

23. Mandeep K. Dhami, "Psychological Models of Professional Decision Making," *Psychological Science* 14, no. 2 (2003): 175–180.

24. Only the prosecution cue was replaced with the cue "Does the defendant have a previous conviction for similar offense?", and if yes, that led to denial of bail.

25. Dhami, "Psychological Models."

26. Dhami, "Psychological Models."

27. Gerd Gigerenzer, *Risk Savvy: How to Make Good Decisions* (New York: Viking, 2014), chap. 3.

28. Dhami, "Psychological Models," 177.

29. Julia Dressel and Hany Farid, "The Accuracy, Fairness, and Limits of Predicting Recidivism," *Science Advances* 4, no. 1 (2018): eaao5580.

30. Jeff Larson et al., "How We Analyzed the COMPAS Recidivism Algorithm," *ProPublica*, May 23, 2016, 5–9.

31. Louis Cook, "The World Trade Center Attack: The Paramedic Response; An Insider's View," *Critical Care* 5, no. 6 (2001): 301–303.

32. Gary Super, *START: A Triage Training Module* (Newport Beach, CA: Hoag Memorial Hospital Presbyterian, 1984). START stands for "simple triage and rapid treatment." The term *triage* is derived from the French verb *trier*, which means to separate, sort, and classify.

33. Lou E. Romig, "Pediatric Triage. A System to JumpSTART Your Triage of Young Patients at MCIs," *Journal of Emergency Medical Services* 27, no. 7 (2002): 52–58.

34. Frank Knight, *Risk, Uncertainty and Profit* (Boston, MA: Houghton Mifflin, 1921).

35. Michael A. Bishop and John D. Trout, *Epistemology and the Psychology of Human Judgment* (New York: Oxford University Press, 2005); Gerd Gigerenzer and Thomas Sturm, "How (Far) Can Rationality Be Naturalized?" *Synthese* 187 (2012): 243–268.

36. Gerd Gigerenzer, "The Bias Bias in Behavioral Economics," *Review of Behavioral Economics*, no. 5 (2018): 303–336.

37. Article 15, EU GDPR, "Right of Access by the Data Subject," http://www.privacy-regulation.eu/en/article-15-right-of-access-by-the-data-subject-GDPR.htm.

38. Advisory Council for Consumer Affairs at the German Federal Ministry of Justice and Consumer Protection. See "Consumer-Friendly Scoring Recommendations for Action," http://www.svr-verbraucherfragen.de/en/wp-content/uploads/sites/2/Recommandations-for-action.pdf.

Chapter 2

1. Michael W. Pozen et al., "A Predictive Instrument to Improve Coronary-Care-Unit Admission Practices in Acute Ischemic Heart Disease: A Prospective Multicenter Clinical Trial," *New England Journal of Medicine* 310, no. 20 (1984): 1273–1278.

2. Lee Green and David R. Mehr, "What Alters Physicians' Decisions to Admit to the Coronary Care Unit?" *Journal of Family Practice* 45, no. 3 (1997): 219–226.

3. Green and Mehr, "What Alters Physicians' Decisions."

4. See articles on this subject at RWI, "Unstatistik des Monats," February 28 and June 7, 2019, http://www.rwi-essen.de/unstatistik.

5. The data were obtained from the authors via personal communication.

6. Mirjam A. Jenny, Niklas Keller, and Gerd Gigerenzer, "Assessing Minimal Medical Statistical Literacy Using the Quick Risk Test: A Prospective Observational Study in Germany," *British Medical Journal Open* 8, no. 8 (2018): e020847.

7. The correct answers to the four questions are 1a, 2b, 3a, and 4b.

8. Quoted by Freeman Dyson in "A Meeting with Enrico Fermi," *Nature* 427 (January 2004): 297.

Chapter 3

1. Lee Green and David Mehr used myocardial infarction (heart attack) as a proxy for ischemic heart disease.

2. David Aikman et al., "Taking Uncertainty Seriously: Simplicity versus Complexity in Financial Regulation," *Industrial and Corporate Change*, in press.

3. Laura Martignon et al., "Naive and Yet Enlightened: From Natural Frequencies to Fast and Frugal Decision Trees," in *Thinking: Psychological Perspectives on Reasoning, Judgment, and Decision Making*, ed. Laura Macchi and David Hardman (Hoboken, NJ: John Wiley and Sons, 2003), 189–211.

4. Martignon et al., "Naive and Yet Enlightened"; Laura Martignon, Konstantinos V. Katsikopoulos, and Jan K. Woike, "Categorization with Limited Resources: A Family of Simple Heuristics," *Journal of Mathematical Psychology* 52, no. 6 (2008): 352–361; Shenghua Luan, Lael J. Schooler, and Gerd Gigerenzer, "A Signal-Detection Analysis of Fast-and-Frugal Trees," *Psychological Review* 118, no. 2 (2011): 316–338.

5. Nathaniel D. Phillips et al., "FFTrees: A Toolbox to Create, Visualize, and Evaluate Fast-and-Frugal Decision Trees," *Judgment and Decision Making* 12, no. 4 (2017): 344–368; "Adaptive Toolbox Library and Tools," http://www.adaptivetoolbox.net/library.

6. Jeffrey S. Simonoff, *Analyzing Categorical Data* (New York: Springer, 2003), chap. 4. The data set can be downloaded from the author's website, accessed December 24, 2019, http://people.stern.nyu.edu/jsimonof/AnalCatData/Data.

7. David A. Hunter, "The Conservation and Demography of the Southern Corroboree Frog" (MA thesis, University of Canberra, 2000). The data are available from the R-package DAAG written by John H. Maindonald and W. John Braun.

8. Tiago A. Almeida, José M. G. Hidalgo, and Akebo Yamakami, "Contributions to the Study of SMS Spam Filtering: New Collection and Results," *Proceedings of the 11th ACM Symposium on Document Engineering* (2011): 259–262. The data set is available from the UCI machine learning repository, https://archive.ics.uci.edu.

9. Yann LeCun et al., "Gradient-Based Learning Applied to Document Recognition," *Proceedings of the IEEE* (1998). The data set can be downloaded from the first author's website, accessed December 24, 2019, http://yann.lecun.com/exdb/mnist.

10. Kory Becker, "Identifying the Gender of a Voice Using Machine Learning," *Primary Objects* (blog), June 22, 2017, accessed December 24, 2019, http://www.primaryobjects.com/2016/06/22/identifying-the-gender-of-a-voice-using-machine-learning.

11. Lennart Grosser, "Sloan Digital Sky Survey DR14," data set contributed to the website kaggle.com, accessed December 24, 2019, https://www.kaggle.com/lucidlenn

/sloan-digital-sky-survey. The data set is based on release 14 of the Sloan Digital Sky Survey, accessed December 24, 2019, http://www.sdss.org/dr14.

12. Luan et al., "Signal-Detection Analysis."

13. Wilson P. Tanner Jr. and John A. Swets, "A Decision-Making Theory of Visual Detection," *Psychological Review* 61, no. 6 (1954): 401–409.

14. Luan et al., "Signal-Detection Analysis."

15. Gerd Gigerenzer, Peter M. Todd, and the ABC Research Group, *Simple Heuristics That Make Us Smart* (New York: Oxford University Press, 1999); Peter M. Todd, Gerd Gigerenzer, and the ABC Research Group, *Ecological Rationality: Intelligence in the World* (New York: Oxford University Press, 2012).

16. Markus Wübben and Florian V. Wangenheim, "Instant Customer Base Analysis: Managerial Heuristics Often 'Get It Right,'" *Journal of Marketing* 72, no. 3 (2008): 82–93.

17. Wübben and Wangenheim, "Instant Customer Base Analysis."

18. Florian Artinger et al., "Recency: Prediction with Smart Data," in *2018 AMA Winter Academic Conference: Integrating Paradigms in a World Where Marketing Is Everywhere*, ed. Jacob Goldenberg, Juliano Laran, and Andrew Stephen (Chicago: American Marketing Association, 2018), 2–6.

19. Gerd Gigerenzer, "What Is Bounded Rationality?" in *Routledge Handbook of Bounded Rationality*, ed. Riccardo Viale (London: Routledge, in press).

20. Martignon et al., "Categorization with Limited Resources."

21. For a proof, see Martignon et al., "Categorization with Limited Resources," 359–360. For similar conditions, see Konstantinos V. Katsikopoulos and Laura Martignon, "Naive Heuristics for Paired Comparisons: Some Results on Their Relative Accuracy," *Journal of Mathematical Psychology* 50, no. 3 (2006): 488–494.

22. Stuart Geman, Elie Bienenstock, and René Doursat, "Neural Networks and the Bias/Variance Dilemma," *Neural Computation* 4, no. 1 (1992): 1–58.

23. Gerd Gigerenzer and Henry Brighton, "Homo Heuristicus: Why Biased Minds Make Better Inferences," *Topics in Cognitive Science* 1, no. 1 (2009): 107–143.

24. Geman, Bienenstock, and Doursat, "Neural Networks."

25. Additional conditions guarantee that fast-and-frugal classifiers have no more bias than more complex classifiers. One such condition is cumulative dominance. See Manel Baucells, Juan A. Carrasco, and Robin M. Hogarth, "Cumulative Dominance and Heuristic Performance in Binary Multiattribute Choice," *Operations Research* 56, no. 5 (2008): 1289–1304; Konstantinos V. Katsikopoulos, "Psychological Heuristics for Making Inferences: Definition, Performance, and the Emerging Theory

and Practice," *Decision Analysis* 8, no. 1 (2011): 10–29; Özgür Şimşek, "Linear Decision Rule as Aspiration for Simple Decision Heuristics," *Advances in Neural Information Processing Systems* (2013): 2904–2912. For a discussion of ecological rationality in other decision tasks, such as multiattribute choice and forecasting, see Konstantinos V. Katsikopoulos, Ian N. Durbach, and Theodor J. Stewart, "When Should We Use Simple Decision Models? A Synthesis of Various Research Strands," *Omega* 81 (2018): 17–25.

Chapter 4

1. Simon Denyer, "China's Watchful Eye," *Washington Post*, January 7, 2018; Christina Larson, "China's AI Imperative: The Country's Massive Investments in Artificial Intelligence Are Disrupting the Industry—and Strengthening Control of the Populace," *Science* 359, no. 6376 (2018): 628–630.

2. Florian Schroff, Dmitry Kalenichenko, and James Philbin, "Facenet: A Unified Embedding for Face Recognition and Clustering," in *Proceedings of the IEEE Conference on Computer Vision and Pattern Recognition*, 2015, 815–823.

3. Neeraj Kumar et al., "Attribute and Simile Classifiers for Face Verification," in *2009 IEEE 12th International Conference on Computer Vision*, 2009, 365–372. In this experiment, 50 percent of the presented pairs showed the same person, and the other 50 percent showed different people.

4. State Council, "Planning Outline for the Construction of a Social Credit System (2014–2020)," *China Copyright and Media*, 2014; Fan Liang et al., "Constructing a Data-Driven Society: China's Social Credit System as a State Surveillance Infrastructure," *Policy and Internet*, August 2, 2018.

5. Human Rights Watch, *China: Police "Big Data" Systems Violate Privacy, Target Dissent*, 2017.

6. Note that 2,297 / 2,470 is not the false alarm rate. The false alarm rate equals the ratio of falsely identified soccer fans to all soccer fans who are not criminals. To compute it, we would need to know how many of the soccer fans were not criminals. If we assume that the face recognition system was perfectly sensitive and did not miss any criminals, then the number of noncriminals equals (170,000 – 2,470) + 2,297 = 169,827. The false alarm rate is 2,297 / 169,827 = 0.014, or 1.4 percent.

7. Gary Marcus and Ernest Davis, "How to Build Artificial Intelligence We Can Trust," *New York Times International Edition*, September 11, 2019.

8. Jennifer Lynch, *Face Off: Law Enforcement Use of Face Recognition Technology*, Electronic Frontier Foundation, February 12, 2018, https://www.eff.org/wp/face-off.

9. Federal Bureau of Investigation, *FBI Criminal Justice Information Services 2016 Annual Report*, 2016.

10. Andre Esteva et al., "Dermatologist-Level Classification of Skin Cancer with Deep Neural Networks," *Nature* 542, no. 7639 (2017): 115.

11. A complication is that the images could be produced by using a variety of technologies (e.g., different medical devices or smartphones), leading to different images for the same mole. In such cases, a fixed classification rule could, depending on the technology used, lead to different decisions for the same mole.

12. US Preventive Services Task Force, "Screening for Skin Cancer: US Preventive Services Task Force Recommendation Statement," *Annals of Internal Medicine* 150, no. 3 (2009): 429.

13. Gilbert H. Welch, Steven Woloshin, and Lisa M. Schwartz, "Skin Biopsy Rates and Incidence of Melanoma: Population-Based Ecological Study," *British Medical Journal* 331, no. 7515 (2005): 481.

14. Vinay Prasad, Jeanne Lenzer, and David H. Newman, "Why Cancer Screening Has Never Been Shown to 'Save Lives'—and What We Can Do about It," *British Medical Journal* 352 (2016): h6080.

15. David Silver et al., "Mastering the Game of Go without Human Knowledge," *Nature* 550, no. 7676 (2017): 354–359.

16. David Silver et al., "A General Reinforcement Learning Algorithm That Masters Chess, Shogi, and Go through Self-Play," *Science* 362, no. 6419 (2018): 1140–1144.

17. World Health Organization, *Influenza Fact Sheet*, 2018, http://www.who.int/en/news-room/fact-sheets/detail/influenza-(seasonal).

18. Neil M. Ferguson et al., "Strategies for Containing an Emerging Influenza Pandemic in Southeast Asia," *Nature* 437, no. 7056 (2005): 209–214.

19. Jeremy Ginsberg et al., "Detecting Influenza Epidemics Using Search Engine Query Data," *Nature* 457, no. 7232 (2009): 1012–1014.

20. Donald R. Olson et al., "Reassessing Google Flu Trends Data for Detection of Seasonal and Pandemic Influenza: A Comparative Epidemiological Study at Three Geographic Scales," *PLOS Computational Biology* 9, no. 10 (2013): e1003256.

21. In fact, the revised Google Flu Trends paper does not give a precise number of cues but says that there were approximately 160 cues.

22. Samantha Cook et al., "Assessing Google Flu Trends Performance in the United States during the 2009 Influenza Virus A (H1N1) Pandemic," *PloS One* 6, no. 8 (2011): e23610.

23. David Lazer et al., "The Parable of Google Flu: Traps in Big Data Analysis," *Science* 343, no. 6176 (2014): 1203–1205.

24. Centers for Disease Control and Prevention, *2009 H1N1 Early Outbreak and Disease Characteristics*, 2009, https://www.cdc.gov/h1n1flu/surveillanceqa.htm.

25. Lazer et al., "The Parable of Google Flu."

26. Ginsberg et al., "Detecting Influenza Epidemics."

27. The website trends.google.com shows how frequently Google's users searched for any term across time.

28. Thomas Brown, *Lectures on the Philosophy of the Human Mind* (London: William Tait, 1838).

29. John R. Anderson and Lael J. Schooler, "Reflections of the Environment in Memory," *Psychological Science* 2, no. 6 (1991): 396–408.

30. CDC FluView Interactive, "National, Regional, and State Level Outpatient Illness and Viral Surveillance," accessed November 11, 2019, https://gis.cdc.gov/grasp/fluview/fluportaldashboard.html.

31. Lazer et al., "The Parable of Google Flu." The regression is discussed not in the main article but in the appendix. Several other models were more accurate than Google Flu Trends. A hybrid linear model that integrates past doctor visits and Google Flu Trends prediction performed best, with a mean absolute error of 0.23 percentage points. This model performs well, but it needs Google Flu Trends in the first place.

32. For more comparisons of performance of big data analytics and simple rules, as well as their hybrids, on out-of-sample and out-of-population predictions, see Sharad Goel et al., "Predicting Consumer Behavior with Web Search," *Proceedings of the National Academy of Sciences* 107, no. 41 (2010): 17486–17490.

33. Gerd Gigerenzer, *Calculated Risk: How to Know When Numbers Deceive You* (New York: Simon and Schuster, 2002).

34. William C. Thompson, Franco Taroni, and Colin G. G. Aitken, "How the Probability of a False Positive Affects the Value of DNA Evidence," *Journal of Forensic Science* 48, no. 1 (2003): 1–8.

35. Lauren Kirchner, "Traces of Crime: How New York's DNA Techniques Became Tainted," *New York Times*, September 4, 2017.

36. Lauren Kirchner, "Where Traditional DNA Testing Fails, Algorithms Take Over," *ProPublica*, November 4, 2016.

37. Article 15, EU GDPR, "Right of Access by the Data Subject," http://www.privacy-regulation.eu/en/article-15-right-of-access-by-the-data-subject-GDPR.htm.

38. Tweet by Pedro Domingos (professor for machine learning at the University of Washington), January 28, 2018: "Starting May 25, the European Union will require algorithms to explain their output, making deep learning illegal."

39. German Advisory Council for Consumer Affairs, *Consumer-Friendly Scoring*, 2019. The recommendation (including one of the authors, GG) that all cues should be revealed to the public was a minority recommendation; the rest of the Advisory Council preferred that only some of the cues be revealed.

40. Cynthia Rudin and Joanna Radin, "Why Are We Using Black Box Models in AI When We Don't Need To? A Lesson from an Explainable AI Competition," *Harvard Data Science Review* 1, no. 2 (2019).

41. Stefan Lessmann et al., "Benchmarking State-of-the-Art Classification Algorithms for Credit Scoring: An Update of Research," *European Journal of Operational Research* 247, no. 1 (2015): 124–136.

42. The precise number of passengers and survivors is not known. We used the data set from Robert J. MacG. Dawson, "The 'Unusual Episode' Data Revisited," *Journal of Statistics Education* 3, no. 3 (1995). It contains the data on 2,201 passengers, of whom 711 survived (32 percent) and 1,490 died (68 percent).

43. Leo Breiman et al., *Classification and Regression Trees* (Boca Raton, FL: CRC Press, 1984).

44. James N. Morgan and John A. Sonquist, "Problems in the Analysis of Survey Data, and a Proposal," *Journal of the American Statistical Association* 58, no. 302 (1963): 415–434.

45. Fast-and-frugal trees can also be constructed by using measures other than Gini impurity, such as positive and negative predictive value or the Best Fit method (chap. 3), as here.

46. To obtain a stable estimate of the performance, we repeated the experiment of randomly drawing 500 voters for training, testing 250 times, and reporting the average classification accuracy.

47. J. Ross Quinlan, *C4.5: Programs for Machine Learning* (Amsterdam, Netherlands: Elsevier, 1993).

48. Ronald L. Rivest, "Learning Decision Lists," *Machine Learning* 2, no. 3 (1987): 229–246.

49. William W. Cohen, "Fast Effective Rule Induction," in *Proceedings of the Twelfth International Conference on Machine Learning* (New York: ACM, 1995), 115–123. RIPPER proceeds as follows: First, a rule is generated so that it fits the training data set with 100 percent accuracy or as close to that as possible. This is achieved by sequentially adding cues to the rule and evaluating accuracy. Note that the rule does

not have to be accurate for all instances, only for the instances to which it applies. Adding cues decreases the number of instances to which the rule applies, which could lead to overfitting. Second, rules are pruned. This is done with the help of a validation data set. The cues in a rule are provisionally removed in the reverse order from the one they were added in the first step (for example, the cue added last is removed first). At each stage of this process, accuracy is evaluated as the ratio $(r - w)/(r + w)$, where r denotes the number of correct classifications and w the number of incorrect classifications of the rule in the validation set. The cues that correspond to the stage with maximum accuracy are retained. More sophisticated pruning methods are also used in RIPPER and other list construction algorithms, including Bayesian approaches.

50. Manuel Fernández-Delgado et al., "Do We Need Hundreds of Classifiers to Solve Real World Classification Problems?" *Journal of Machine Learning Research* 15, no. 1 (2014): 3133–3181.

51. Benjamin Letham et al., "Interpretable Classifiers Using Rules and Bayesian Analysis: Building a Better Stroke Prediction Model," *Annals of Applied Statistics* 9, no. 3 (2015): 1350–1371.

52. Elliott M. Antman et al., "The TIMI Risk Score for Unstable Angina / Non-ST Elevation MI: A Method for Prognostication and Therapeutic Decision Making," *Journal of the American Medical Association* 284, no. 7 (2000): 835–842.

53. Sihai Dave Zhao et al., "Más-o-Menos: A Simple Sign Averaging Method for Discrimination in Genomic Data Analysis," *Bioinformatics* 30, no. 21 (2014): 3062–3069.

54. Yann Chevaleyre, Frédéric Koriche, and Jean-Daniel Zucker, "Rounding Methods for Discrete Linear Classification," in *Proceedings of the 30th International Conference on International Conference on Machine Learning* (Atlanta: JMLR.org, 2013), 651–659.

55. Marcus Buckmann and Özgür Şimşek, *Learning Interpretable Models* (Berlin: Working Paper, 2019).

56. Jack W. Smith et al., "Using the ADAP Learning Algorithm to Forecast the Onset of Diabetes Mellitus," in *Proceedings of the Annual Symposium on Computer Application in Medical Care* (American Medical Informatics Association, 1988), 261.

57. Applying the Best Fit method can be computationally extremely demanding, especially in data sets with many numeric cues. As an approximation, we used the cross-entropy method; see Reuven Rubinstein, "The Cross-Entropy Method for Combinatorial and Continuous Optimization," *Methodology and Computing in Applied Probability* 1, no. 2 (1999): 127–190. This method does not guarantee finding the one fast-and-frugal tree that fits best, but on average it produces highly accurate fast-and-frugal trees.

58. Maciej Zięba, Sebastian K. Tomczak, and Jakub M. Tomczak, "Ensemble Boosted Trees with Synthetic Features Generation in Application to Bankruptcy Prediction," *Expert Systems with Applications* 58 (2016): 93–101.

59. Unlike CART, random forests, which are highly nontransparent in their logic, tend to confuse practitioners. We nevertheless calculated what predictive advantage random forests would gain over CART. For the same sixty-four tasks, random forests predicted better than the heuristics on average; their balanced error was 3.3 percentage points lower. On the other hand, in thirteen of the tasks, tallying or fast-and-frugal trees performed as well as or better than random forests. As usual, the frugality of random forests was orders of magnitude worse than that of fast-and-frugal classifiers.

60. Rudin and Radin, "Why Are We Using Black Box Models."

Chapter 5

1. Paul C. Quinn, Peter D. Eimas, and Michael J. Tarr, "Perceptual Categorization of Cat and Dog Silhouettes by 3- to 4-Month-Old Infants," *Journal of Experimental Child Psychology* 79, no. 1 (2001): 78–94.

2. David H. Rakison and Lisa M. Oakes, eds., *Early Category and Concept Development: Making Sense of the Blooming, Buzzing Confusion* (Oxford: Oxford University Press, 2003).

3. Brenden M. Lake et al., "Building Machines That Learn and Think Like People," *Behavioral and Brain Sciences* 40 (2017): e253.

4. Egon Brunswik is a notable exception. During the 1940s and 1950s, he transformed Hermann von Helmholtz's notion of unconscious inferences into linear multiple regression. Yet Brunswik treated regression as an as-if model, not as a model of the actual cognitive processes. At the time, his theory was rejected by most of his fellow experimental psychologists, who could make little sense of the analogy between the perceptual system and a statistician.

5. Gerd Gigerenzer and David J. Murray, *Cognition as Intuitive Statistics* (London: Psychology Press, 2015).

6. Wilson P. Tanner Jr. and John A. Swets, "A Decision-Making Theory of Visual Detection," *Psychological Review* 61, no. 6 (1954): 401–409.

7. Gigerenzer and Murray, *Cognition as Intuitive Statistics.*

8. Gerd Gigerenzer, "From Tools to Theories: A Heuristic of Discovery in Cognitive Psychology," *Psychological Review* 98, no. 2 (1991): 254–267.

9. Jerome S. Bruner, Jacqueline J. Goodnow, and George A. Austin, *A Study of Thinking* (New York: John Wiley and Sons, 1956).

10. Gerd Gigerenzer, "Ideas in Exile: The Struggles of an Upright Man," in *The Essential Brunswik: Beginnings, Explications, Applications*, ed. Kenneth R. Hammond and Tom R. Stewart (Oxford: Oxford University Press, 2001), 445–452.

11. The distinction between artificial and natural objects is not a categorical one; there are many intermediary degrees.

12. Michael Allen, "Preschool Children's Taxonomic Knowledge of Animal Species," *Journal of Research in Science Teaching* 52, no. 1 (2015): 107–134.

13. Herbert A. Simon, "Rational Choice and the Structure of the Environment," *Psychological Review* 63, no. 2 (1956): 129–138.

14. Gerd Gigerenzer and Reinhard Selten, eds., *Bounded Rationality: The Adaptive Toolbox* (Cambridge, MA: MIT Press, 2001).

15. Pawan Sinha et al., *Face Recognition: Models and Mechanism* (Cambridge, MA: Academic Press, 2003).

16. Sinha et al., *Face Recognition*.

17. Kevin J. Ford et al., "Process Tracing Methods: Contributions, Problems, and Neglected Research Questions," *Organizational Behavior and Human Decision Processes* 43, no. 1 (1989): 75–117; John W. Payne, James R. Bettman, and Eric J. Johnson, *The Adaptive Decision Maker* (Cambridge: Cambridge University Press, 1993).

18. John M. C. Hutchinson and Gerd Gigerenzer, "Simple Heuristics and Rules of Thumb: Where Psychologists and Behavioural Biologists Might Meet," *Behavioural Processes* 69, no. 2 (2005): 97–124.

19. Tobias Dantzig, *Number, the Language of Science: A Critical Survey Written for the Cultured Non-Mathematician* (London: Penguin, 1954).

20. Dantzig, *Number, the Language of Science*.

21. Thomas Åstebro and Samir Elhedhli, "The Effectiveness of Simple Decision Heuristics: Forecasting Commercial Success for Early-Stage Ventures," *Management Science* 52, no. 3 (2006): 395–409; Jan K. Woike, Ulrich Hoffrage, and Jeffrey S. Petty, "Picking Profitable Investments: The Success of Equal Weighting in Simulated Venture Capitalist Decision Making," *Journal of Business Research* 68, no. 8 (2015): 1705–1716.

22. Victor DeMiguel, Lorenzo Garlappi, and Raman Uppal, "Optimal versus Naive Diversification: How Inefficient Is the 1/N Portfolio Strategy?" *Review of Financial Studies* 22, no. 5 (2007): 1915–1953.

23. Ralph Hertwig, Jennifer Nerissa Davis, and Frank J. Sulloway, "Parental Investment: How an Equity Motive Can Produce Inequality," *Psychological Bulletin* 128, no. 5 (2002): 728–745.

24. Jolene H. Tan, Shenghua Luan, and Konstantinos V. Katsikopoulos, "A Signal-Detection Approach to Modeling Forgiveness Decisions," *Evolution and Human Behavior* 38, no. 1 (2017): 27–38.

25. Robyn M. Dawes, "The Robust Beauty of Improper Linear Models in Decision Making," *American Psychologist* 34, no. 7 (1979): 571–582; Robyn M. Dawes and Bernard Corrigan, "Linear Models in Decision Making," *Psychological Bulletin* 81, no. 2 (1974): 95–106.

26. Dawes, "Robust Beauty," 577.

27. Hillel J. Einhorn and Robin M. Hogarth, "Unit Weighting Schemes for Decision Making," *Organizational Behavior and Human Performance* 13, no. 2 (1975): 171–192.

28. Leo Breiman, "Statistical Modeling: The Two Cultures (with Comments and a Rejoinder by the Author)," *Statistical Science* 16, no. 3 (2001): 199–231.

29. Jean Czerlinski, Gerd Gigerenzer, and Daniel G. Goldstein, "How Good Are Simple Heuristics?" in *Simple Heuristics That Make Us Smart*, by Gerd Gigerenzer, Peter M. Todd, and the ABC Research Group (New York: Oxford University Press, 1999), 97–118.

30. Gerd Gigerenzer and Daniel G. Goldstein, "Reasoning the Fast and Frugal Way: Models of Bounded Rationality," *Psychological Review*, no. 103 (1996): 650–669.

31. Robin M. Hogarth, "When Simple Is Hard to Accept," in *Ecological Rationality: Intelligence in the World*, by Peter M. Todd, Gerd Gigerenzer, and the ABC Research Group (Oxford: Oxford University Press, 2012), 61–79.

32. Mininder S. Kocher et al., "Validation of a Clinical Prediction Rule for the Differentiation between Septic Arthritis and Transient Synovitis of the Hip in Children," *Journal of Bone and Joint Surgery* 86, no. 8 (2004): 1629–1635.

33. Elliott M. Antman et al., "The TIMI Risk Score for Unstable Angina / Non-ST Elevation MI: A Method for Prognostication and Therapeutic Decision Making," *Journal of the American Medical Association* 284, no. 7 (2000): 835–842.

34. Christopher W. Seymour et al., "Assessment of Clinical Criteria for Sepsis for the Third International Consensus Definitions for Sepsis and Septic Shock (Sepsis-3)," *Journal of the American Medical Association* 315, no. 8 (2016): 762–774.

35. Ron Pisters et al., "A Novel User-Friendly Score (HAS-BLED) to Assess 1-Year Risk of Major Bleeding in Patients with Atrial Fibrillation: The Euro Heart Survey," *Chest* 138, no. 5 (2010): 1093–1100.

36. Vanja C. Douglas et al., "The AWOL Tool: Derivation and Validation of a Delirium Prediction Rule," *Journal of Hospital Medicine* 8, no. 9 (2013): 493–499.

37. Wei S. Lim et al., "Defining Community Acquired Pneumonia Severity on Presentation to Hospital: An International Derivation and Validation Study," *Thorax* 58, no. 5 (2003): 377–382.

38. Amos Tversky, "Elimination by Aspects: A Theory of Choice," *Psychological Review* 79, no. 4 (1972): 281–299.

39. Arndt Bröder, "The Quest for Take-the-Best," in *Ecological Rationality: Intelligence in the World*, ed. Peter M. Todd, Gerd Gigerenzer, and the ABC Research Group (New York: Oxford University Press, 2012), 216–240.

40. Özgür Şimşek and Marcus Buckmann, "Learning from Small Samples: An Analysis of Simple Decision Heuristics," in *Advances in Neural Information Processing Systems* 28 (2015): 3159–3167; Marcus Buckmann and Özgür Şimşek, "Decision Heuristics for Comparison: How Good Are They?" *Proceedings of the NIPS 2016 Workshop on Imperfect Decision Makers*, in *PMLR* 58 (2017): 1–11.

41. Amos Tversky and Daniel Kahneman, "Judgment under Uncertainty: Heuristics and Biases," *Science* 185, no. 4157 (1974): 1124–1131.

42. Gigerenzer, Todd, and ABC Research Group, *Simple Heuristics That Make Us Smart*; Gerd Gigerenzer, Ralph Hertwig, and Thorsten Pachur, eds., *Heuristics: The Foundations of Adaptive Behavior* (New York: Oxford University Press, 2011).

43. Liz Smith and Ken Gilhooly, "Regression versus Fast and Frugal Models of Decision-Making: The Case of Prescribing for Depression," *Applied Cognitive Psychology: The Official Journal of the Society for Applied Research in Memory and Cognition* 20, no. 2 (2006): 265–274.

44. Mandeep K. Dhami and Clare Harries, "Information Search in Heuristic Decision Making," *Applied Cognitive Psychology: The Official Journal of the Society for Applied Research in Memory and Cognition* 24, no. 4 (2010): 571–586.

45. Lars G. Backlund et al., "Improving Fast and Frugal Modeling in Relation to Regression Analysis: Test of 3 Models for Medical Decision Making," *Medical Decision Making* 29, no. 1 (2009): 140–148.

46. Joachim E. Fischer et al., "Use of Simple Heuristics to Target Macrolide Prescription in Children with Community-Acquired Pneumonia," *Archives of Pediatrics and Adolescent Medicine* 156, no. 10 (2002): 1005–1008.

47. Mirjam A. Jenny et al., "Simple Rules for Detecting Depression," *Journal of Applied Research in Memory and Cognition* 2, no. 3 (2013): 149–157.

48. Benjamin Djulbegovic, Iztok Hozo, and William Dale, "Transforming Clinical Practice Guidelines and Clinical Pathways into Fast-and-Frugal Decision Trees to

Improve Clinical Care Strategies," *Journal of Evaluation in Clinical Practice* 24, no. 5 (2018): 1247–1254.

49. Aanand D. Naik et al., "A Fast and Frugal Algorithm to Strengthen Diagnosis and Treatment Decisions for Catheter-Associated Bacteriuria," *PLOS One* 12, no. 3 (2017): e0174415.

50. Nathan Davies et al., "Guiding Practitioners through End of Life Care for People with Dementia: The Use of Heuristics," *PLOS One* 13, no. 11 (2018): e0206422.

51. Tibor van Rooij et al., "Fast and Frugal Trees: Translating Population-Based Pharmacogenomics to Medication Prioritization," *Personalized Medicine* 12, no. 2 (2015): 117–128.

52. Shenghua Luan and Jochen Reb, "Fast-and-Frugal Trees as Noncompensatory Models of Performance-Based Personnel Decisions," *Organizational Behavior and Human Decision Processes* 141 (2017): 29–42.

53. Merkourios Karaliopoulos and Iordanis Koutsopoulos, "Mobile App User Choice Engineering Using Behavioral Science Models," in *2018 IEEE 19th International Workshop on Signal Processing Advances in Wireless Communications* (Piscataway: IEEE, 2018): 1–5.

54. Merkourios Karaliopoulos, Konstantinos V. Katsikopoulos, and Lambros Lambrinos, "Bounded Rationality Can Make Parking Search More Efficient: The Power of Lexicographic Heuristics," *Transportation Research Part B: Methodological* 101 (2017): 28–50.

55. Adapted from experiment 1 of Douglas L. Medin and Marguerite M. Schaffer, "Context Theory of Classification Learning," *Psychological Review* 85, no. 3 (1978): 207–238.

56. John K. Kruschke, "Models of Categorization," in *The Cambridge Handbook of Computational Psychology*, ed. Ron Sun (New York: Cambridge University Press, 2008).

57. Gregory F. Ashby and Leola A. Alfonso-Reese, "Categorization as Probability Density Estimation," *Journal of Mathematical Psychology* 39, no. 2 (1995): 216–233.

58. Some cognitive scientists have argued that "Bayesian brains" can work "without probabilities"; see, e.g., Adam N. Sanborn and Nick Chater, "Bayesian Brains without Probabilities," *Trends in Cognitive Sciences* 20, no. 12 (2016): 883–893. This means that one can estimate probabilities by sampling. That might be true but presupposes that uncertainty in the world can be represented by probabilities, which is not the case in the wild.

59. The hypothesis that exemplars are represented as points in k-dimensional space has been inspired by the technology of (nonmetric) multidimensional scaling. This

tool uses a similarity measure (Euclidean, city block, or another Minkowski metric) to represent objects in multidimensional space. Here we have another case where the tools-to-theories heuristic inspired psychological theorizing.

60. Abraham Wald, *Statistical Decision Functions* (New York: Wiley, 1950).

61. Robert M. Nosofsky and Thomas J. Palmeri, "An Exemplar-Based Random Walk Model of Speeded Classification," *Psychological Review* 104, no. 2 (1997): 266–300.

62. Mario Fific, Daniel R. Little, and Robert M. Nosofsky, "Logical-Rule Models of Classification Response Times: A Synthesis of Mental-Architecture, Random-Walk, and Decision-Bound Approaches," *Psychological Review* 117, no. 2 (2010): 309–348.

63. Andrew L. Cohen and Robert M. Nosofsky, "An Extension of the Exemplar-Based Random-Walk Model to Separable-Dimension Stimuli," *Journal of Mathematical Psychology* 47, no. 2 (2003): 150–165.

64. Jerome R. Busemeyer and Adele Diederich, *Cognitive Modeling* (Thousand Oaks, CA: Sage, 2014).

65. One might respond that stochastic cognitive processes that are not memoryless can also be formulated as memoryless Markov chains / random walks, as long as the system state is redefined appropriately. Although this solution is possible in principle, it is vulnerable to being intractable because it would ultimately require an extremely large number of fine-grained states. An intractable computation cannot be psychologically plausible. Of course, it is not entirely clear whether a Markov process, and the associated computations needed to describe and control it, is indeed intractable. One can nevertheless reasonably assume that the larger a state space is, the more likely it is that the associated computation will be intractable for a human brain.

66. See Robert M. Nosofsky, Thomas J. Palmeri, and Stephen C. McKinley, "Rule-Plus-Exception Model of Classification Learning," *Psychological Review* 101, no. 1 (1994): 53: "It is reasonable to question the plausibility of exemplar storage processes and the vast memory resources they seem to require."

67. For example, RULEX models.

68. Gigerenzer, "From Tools to Theories."

69. Clark Glymour, "Osiander's Psychology," *Behavioral and Brain Sciences* 34, no. 4 (2011): 200.

70. Seth Roberts and Harold Pashler, "How Persuasive Is a Good Fit? A Comment on Theory Testing," *Psychological Review* 107, no. 2 (2000): 358–367; Mark A. Pitt and In Jae Myung, "When a Good Fit Can Be Bad," *Trends in Cognitive Sciences* 6, no. 10 (2002): 421–425.

71. Alan Musgrave, "Logical versus Historical Theories of Confirmation," *British Journal for the Philosophy of Science* 25, no. 1 (1974): 1–23. For a Bayesian analysis of this approach, see David Trafimow, "Hypothesis Testing and Theory Evaluation at the Boundaries: Surprising Insights from Bayes's Theorem," *Psychological Review* 110, no. 3 (2003): 526–535. For general comments, see Konstantinos V. Katsikopoulos, "How to Model It: Review of 'Cognitive Modeling,'" *Journal of Mathematical Psychology* 55, no. 2 (2011): 198–201.

72. Lee W. Gregg and Herbert A. Simon, "Process Models and Stochastic Theories of Simple Concept Formation," *Journal of Mathematical Psychology* 4, no. 2 (1967): 246–276.

73. Gigerenzer and Selten, *Bounded Rationality*.

74. Paul C. Quinn, "Beyond Prototypes," in *Advances in Child Development and Behavior*, ed. Robert V. Kail and Hayne W. Reese (San Diego: Academic Press, 2002), 161–193.

Chapter 6

1. Jeffrey Skiles, interview by Charlie Rose, February 10, 2009, https://charlierose.com/videos/14176?autoplay=true.

2. Gerd Gigerenzer, *Gut Feelings: The Intelligence of the Unconscious* (New York: Penguin, 2007); Robert P. Hamlin, "The Gaze Heuristic: Biography of an Adaptively Rational Decision Process," *Topics in Cognitive Science* 9, no. 2 (2017): 264–288.

3. Kim Sterelny, *Thought in a Hostile World: The Evolution of Human Cognition* (Hoboken, NJ: Wiley Blackwell, 2003).

4. Laurie R. Blank and Amos N. Guiora, "Updating the Commander's Toolbox: New Tools for Operationalizing the Law of Armed Conflict," *Prism* 1, no. 3 (2010): 59–78.

5. Sarah Holewinski, "Escalation of Force: The Civilian Perspective," in *Escalation of Force Handbook* (Fort Leavenworth, KS: Center for Army Lessons Learned, 2007), 81–82.

6. Blank and Guiora, "Updating the Commander's Toolbox."

7. "Petraeus Issues New Directive for Troops in Afghanistan," CNN.com, August 4, 2010, https://www.cnn.com/2010/WORLD/asiapcf/08/04/afghanistan.petraeus/index.html.

8. For example, in close air support such as air strikes, the civilian death toll in Afghanistan decreased from 359 in 2009 to 170 in 2010 and 187 in 2011; see United Nations Assistance Mission to Afghanistan, *Human Rights' Group Annual Report on the Protection of Civilians in Armed Conflict* (Kabul, Afghanistan, 2012).

9. Derek I. Grimes et al., *Operational Law Handbook* (Charlottesville, VA: International and Operational Law Department, Judge Advocate General's Legal Center and School, 2006).

10. Niklas Keller and Konstantinos V. Katsikopoulos, "On the Role of Psychological Heuristics in Operational Research; and a Demonstration in Military Stability Operations," *European Journal of Operational Research* 249, no. 3 (2016): 1063–1073.

11. Keller and Katsikopoulos, "On the Role of Psychological Heuristics."

12. Randall Bagwell, "The Threat Assessment Process," *Army Lawyer*, Department of the Army pamphlet 27-50-419 (2008), 5–16.

13. Nancy Montgomery, "U.S. Seeks to Reduce Civilian Deaths at Iraq Checkpoints," *Stars and Stripes*, March 18, 2006.

14. Briefly available on WikiLeaks in 2010. *Afghanistan War Diaries*, accessed July 29, 2010, http://wikileaks.org/wiki/Afghan_War_Diary,_2004-2010.

15. Bruce Bower, "Decision Tree for Soldiers Could Reduce Civilian Deaths," *Science News*, August 10, 2015, https://www.sciencenews.org/article/decision-tree-soldiers-could-reduce-civilian-deaths.

16. Andrew G. Haldane, "The Dog and the Frisbee," https://www.bis.org/review/r120905a.pdf.

17. Jason Zweig, "The Jackson Hole Speech People Should Long Remember," *Wall Street Journal*, August 31, 2012, https://blogs.wsj.com/totalreturn/2012/08/31/the-jackson-hole-speech-people-should-long-remember.

18. Andrew G. Haldane and Vasileios Madouros, "The Dog and the Frisbee," *Revista de Economia Institucional,* no. 14 (2012): 109–110.

19. David Aikman et al., "Taking Uncertainty Seriously: Simplicity versus Complexity in Financial Regulation," *Industrial and Corporate Change*, in press.

20. Peter Thal Larsen, "Goldman Pays the Price of Being Big," *Financial Times*, March 13, 2007.

21. Anat Admati and Martin Hellwig, *The Bankers' New Clothes: What's Wrong with Banking and What to Do about It* (Princeton, NJ: Princeton University Press, 2014).

22. Joseph E. Stiglitz, *Freefall: America, Free Markets, and the Sinking of the World Economy* (New York: W. W. Norton, 2010).

23. Philipp Härle et al., "Basel III and European Banking: Its Impact, How Banks Might Respond, and the Challenges of Implementation," *EMEA Banking* (2010): 16–17.

24. "Finance and Risk: On Knowing Too Much," *Guardian*, September 9, 2012, https://www.theguardian.com/commentisfree/2012/sep/09/finance-risk-knowing -too-much.

25. Aikman et al., "Taking Uncertainty Seriously."

26. John Wilder Tukey, *Exploratory Data Analysis* (Boston, MA: Addison-Wesley, 1970).

27. Each cue's threshold was chosen so as to minimize Pr[false alarm]–Pr[hit] for that cue.

28. Aikman et al., "Taking Uncertainty Seriously."

29. Admati and Hellwig, *The Bankers' New Clothes*; William P. Forbes, Aloysius Obinna Igboekwu, and Shabnam Mousavi, *A Fast and Frugal Finance: Bridging Contemporary Behavioral Finance and Ecological Rationality* (Cambridge: Academic Press, 2019); John Kay and Mervyn King, *Radical Uncertainty: Decision-Making Beyond the Numbers* (New York: W. W. Norton, 2020).

30. Gerd Gigerenzer, "The Heuristics Revolution: Rethinking the Role of Uncertainty in Finance," in *The Behavioral Finance Revolution: A New Approach to Financial Policies and Regulations*, ed. Riccardo Viale et al. (Cheltenham: Edward Elgar, 2018), 115–134.

31. Nassim Nicholas Taleb, *Skin in the Game: Hidden Asymmetries in Daily Life* (New York: Allen Lane, 2018).

Chapter 7

1. Michael Pollan, *Food Rules: An Eater's Manual* (New York: Penguin, 2009).

2. Gerd Gigerenzer, *Risk Savvy: How to Make Good Decisions* (New York: Viking, 2014).

3. See also Cynthia Rudin, "The Problem with Black Boxes," TWIML Talk no. 290 (podcast), August 12, 2019, https://twimlai.com/twiml-talk-290-the-problem-with -black-boxes-with-cynthia-rudin.

Bibliography

Admati, Anat, and Martin Hellwig. *The Bankers' New Clothes: What's Wrong with Banking and What to Do about It.* Princeton, NJ: Princeton University Press, 2014.

Aikman, David, Mirta Galesic, Gerd Gigerenzer, Sujit Kapadia, Konstantinos V. Katsikopoulos, Amit Kothiyal, Emma Murphy, and Tobias Neumann. "Taking Uncertainty Seriously: Simplicity versus Complexity in Financial Regulation." *Industrial and Corporate Change*, in press.

Allen, Michael. "Preschool Children's Taxonomic Knowledge of Animal Species." *Journal of Research in Science Teaching* 52, no. 1 (2015): 107–134.

Almeida, Tiago A., José M. G. Hidalgo, and Akebo Yamakami. "Contributions to the Study of SMS Spam Filtering: New Collection and Results." *Proceedings of the 11th ACM Symposium on Document Engineering* (2011): 259–262.

Anderson, John R., and Lael J. Schooler. "Reflections of the Environment in Memory." *Psychological Science* 2, no. 6 (1991): 396–408.

Antman, Elliott M., Marc Cohen, Peter J. L. M. Bernink, Carolyn H. McCabe, Thomas Horacek, et al. "The TIMI Risk Score for Unstable Angina/Non-ST Elevation MI: A Method for Prognostication and Therapeutic Decision Making." *Journal of the American Medical Association* 284, no. 7 (2000): 835–842.

Artinger, Florian, Nikita Kozodi, Florian von Wangenheim, and Gerd Gigerenzer. "Recency: Prediction with Smart Data." In *2018 AMA Winter Academic Conference: Integrating Paradigms in a World Where Marketing Is Everywhere*, ed. Jacob Goldenberg, Juliano Laran, and Andrew Stephen, 2–6. Chicago: American Marketing Association, 2018.

Ashby, Gregory F., and Leola A. Alfonso-Reese. "Categorization as Probability Density Estimation." *Journal of Mathematical Psychology* 39, no. 2 (1995): 216–233.

Åstebro, Thomas, and Samir Elhedhli. "The Effectiveness of Simple Decision Heuristics: Forecasting Commercial Success for Early-Stage Ventures." *Management Science* 52, no. 3 (2006): 395–409.

Backlund, Lars G., Johan Bring, Ylva Skånér, Lars-Erik Strender, and Henry Mont-gomery. "Improving Fast and Frugal Modeling in Relation to Regression Analysis: Test of 3 Models for Medical Decision Making." *Medical Decision Making* 29, no. 1 (2009): 140–148.

Bagwell, Randall. "The Threat Assessment Process." *Army Lawyer*. Department of the Army pamphlet 27-50-419 (2008), 5–16.

Baucells, Manel, Juan A. Carrasco, and Robin M. Hogarth. "Cumulative Dominance and Heuristic Performance in Binary Multiattribute Choice." *Operations Research* 56, no. 5 (2008): 1289–1304.

Bishop, Michael A., and John D. Trout. *Epistemology and the Psychology of Human Judgment*. New York: Oxford University Press, 2005.

Blank, Laurie R., and Amos N. Guiora. "Updating the Commander's Toolbox: New Tools for Operationalizing the Law of Armed Conflict." *Prism* 1, no. 3 (2010): 59–78.

Breiman, Leo. "Statistical Modeling: The Two Cultures (with Comments and a Rejoinder by the Author)." *Statistical Science* 16, no. 3 (2001): 199–231.

Breiman, Leo, Jerome Friedman, Charles J. Stone, and Richard A. Olshen. *Classifica-tion and Regression Trees*. Boca Raton, FL: CRC Press, 1984.

Brown, Thomas. *Lectures on the Philosophy of the Human Mind*. London: William Tait, 1838.

Bröder, Arndt. "The Quest for Take-the-Best." In *Ecological Rationality: Intelligence in the World*, ed. Peter M. Todd, Gerd Gigerenzer, and the ABC Research Group, 216–240. New York: Oxford University Press, 2012.

Bruner, Jerome S., Jacqueline J. Goodnow, and George A. Austin. *A Study of Thinking*. New York: John Wiley and Sons, 1956.

Buckmann, Marcus, and Özgür Şimşek. "Decision Heuristics for Comparison: How Good Are They?" *Proceedings of the NIPS 2016 Workshop on Imperfect Decision Makers*, in *PMLR* 58 (2017): 1–11.

Buckmann, Marcus, and Özgür Şimşek. *Learning Interpretable Models*. Berlin: Working Paper, 2019.

Busemeyer, Jerome R., and Adele Diederich. *Cognitive Modeling*. Thousand Oaks, CA: Sage, 2014.

Chevaleyre, Yann, Frédéric Koriche, and Jean-Daniel Zucker. "Rounding Methods for Discrete Linear Classification." In *Proceedings of the 30th International Conference on International Conference on Machine Learning*, 651–659 (Atlanta: JMLR.org, 2013).

Chou, Roger, Laurie Hoyt Huffman, Rongwei Fu, Ariel K. Smits, and P. Todd Korthuis. "Screening for HIV: A Review of the Evidence for the US Preventive Services Task Force." *Annals of Internal Medicine* 143, no. 1 (2005): 55–73.

Cohen, Andrew L., and Robert M. Nosofsky. "An Extension of the Exemplar-Based Random-Walk Model to Separable-Dimension Stimuli." *Journal of Mathematical Psychology* 47, no. 2 (2003): 150–165.

Cohen, William H. "Fast Effective Rule Induction." In *Proceedings of the Twelfth International Conference on Machine Learning*, 115–123 (New York: ACM, 1995).

Converse, Philip E. "The Nature of Belief Systems in Mass Publics." In *Ideology and Discontent*, ed. David Apter, 206–261. New York: Free Press, 1964.

Cook, Louis. "The World Trade Center Attack: The Paramedic Response; An Insider's View." *Critical Care* 5, no. 6 (2001): 301–303.

Cook, Samantha, Corrie Conrad, Ashley L. Fowlkes, and Matthew H. Mohebbi. "Assessing Google Flu Trends Performance in the United States during the 2009 Influenza Virus A (H1N1) Pandemic." *PloS One* 6, no. 8 (2011): e23610.

Czerlinski, Jean, Gerd Gigerenzer, and Daniel G. Goldstein. "How Good Are Simple Heuristics?" In *Simple Heuristics That Make Us Smart*, by Gerd Gigerenzer, Peter M. Todd, and the ABC Research Group, 97–118. New York: Oxford University Press, 1999.

Dantzig, Tobias. *Number, the Language of Science: A Critical Survey Written for the Cultured Non-Mathematician*. London: Penguin, 1954.

Davies, Nathan, Jill Manthorpe, Elizabeth L. Sampson, Kethakie Lamahewa, Jane Wilcock, Rammya Mathew, and Steve Iliffe. "Guiding Practitioners through End of Life Care for People with Dementia: The Use of Heuristics." *PLOS One* 13, no. 11 (2018): e0206422.

Dawes, Robyn M. "The Robust Beauty of Improper Linear Models in Decision Making." *American Psychologist* 34, no. 7 (1979): 571–582.

Dawes, Robyn M., and Bernard Corrigan. "Linear Models in Decision Making." *Psychological Bulletin* 81, no. 2 (1974): 95–106.

Dawson, Robert J. MacG. "The 'Unusual Episode' Data Revisited." *Journal of Statistics Education* 3, no. 3 (1995).

DeMiguel, Victor, Lorenzo Garlappi, and Raman Uppal. "Optimal versus Naive Diversification: How Inefficient Is the 1/N Portfolio Strategy?" *Review of Financial Studies* 22, no. 5 (2007): 1915–1953.

Dhami, Mandeep K. "Psychological Models of Professional Decision Making." *Psychological Science* 14, no. 2 (2003): 175–180.

Dhami, Mandeep K., and Peter Ayton. "Bailing and Jailing the Fast and Frugal Way." *Journal of Behavioral Decision Making* 14, no. 2 (2001): 141–168.

Dhami, Mandeep K., and Clare Harries. "Information Search in Heuristic Decision Making." *Applied Cognitive Psychology: The Official Journal of the Society for Applied Research in Memory and Cognition* 24, no. 4 (2010): 571–586.

Djulbegovic, Benjamin, Iztok Hozo, and William Dale. "Transforming Clinical Practice Guidelines and Clinical Pathways into Fast-and-Frugal Decision Trees to Improve Clinical Care Strategies." *Journal of Evaluation in Clinical Practice* 24, no. 5 (2018): 1247–1254.

Douglas, Vanja C., Christine S. Hessler, Gurpreet Dhaliwal, John P. Betjemann, Keiko A. Fukuda, Lama R. Alameddine, Rachael Lucatorto, et al. "The AWOL Tool: Derivation and Validation of a Delirium Prediction Rule." *Journal of Hospital Medicine* 8, no. 9 (2013): 493–499.

Doyle, Nora M., Judy E. Levinson, and Michael O. Gardner. "Rapid versus Enzyme-Linked Immunosorbent Assay Screening in a Low-Risk Mexican American Population Presenting in Labor: A Cost-Effectiveness Analysis." *American Journal of Obstetrics and Gynecology* 193, no. 5 (2005): 1280–1285.

Dressel, Julia, and Hany Farid. "The Accuracy, Fairness, and Limits of Predicting Recidivism." *Science Advances* 4, no. 1 (2018): eaao5580.

Dyson, Freeman. "A Meeting with Enrico Fermi." *Nature* 427 (January 2004): 297.

Einhorn, Hillel J., and Robin M. Hogarth. "Unit Weighting Schemes for Decision Making." *Organizational Behavior and Human Performance* 13, no. 2 (1975): 171–192.

Estes, William K. *Classification and Cognition.* New York: Oxford University Press, 1994.

Esteva, Andre, Brett Kuprel, Roberto A. Novoa, Justin Ko, Susan M. Swetter, Helen M. Blau, and Sebastian Thrun. "Dermatologist-Level Classification of Skin Cancer with Deep Neural Networks." *Nature* 542, no. 7639 (2017): 115.

Federal Bureau of Investigation. *FBI Criminal Justice Information Services 2016 Annual Report.* 2016.

Ferguson, Neal M., Derek A. T. Cummings, Simon Cauchemez, Christophe Fraser, Steven Riley, Aronrag Meeyai, et al. "Strategies for Containing an Emerging Influenza Pandemic in Southeast Asia." *Nature* 437, no. 7056 (2005): 209–214.

Fernández-Delgado, Manuel, Eva Cernadas, Senén Barro, and Dinani Amorim. "Do We Need Hundreds of Classifiers to Solve Real World Classification Problems?" *Journal of Machine Learning Research* 15, no. 1 (2014): 3133–3181.

Fific, Mario, Daniel R. Little, and Robert M. Nosofsky. "Logical-Rule Models of Classification Response Times: A Synthesis of Mental-Architecture, Random-Walk, and Decision-Bound Approaches." *Psychological Review* 117, no. 2 (2010): 309–348.

Fischer, Joachim E., Felicitas Steiner, Franziska Zucol, Christoph Berger, Laura Martignon, Walter Bossart, Martin Altwegg, and David Nadal. "Use of Simple Heuristics to Target Macrolide Prescription in Children with Community-Acquired Pneumonia." *Archives of Pediatrics and Adolescent Medicine* 156, no. 10 (2002): 1005–1008.

Forbes, William P., Aloysius Obinna Igboekwu, and Shabnam Mousavi. *A Fast and Frugal Finance: Bridging Contemporary Behavioral Finance and Ecological Rationality*. Cambridge: Academic Press, 2019.

Ford, Kevin J., Neal Schmitt, Susan L. Schechtman, Brian M. Hults, and Mary L. Doherty. "Process Tracing Methods: Contributions, Problems, and Neglected Research Questions." *Organizational Behavior and Human Decision Processes* 43, no. 1 (1989): 75–117.

Geman, Stuart, Elie Bienenstock, and René Doursat. "Neural Networks and the Bias/ Variance Dilemma." *Neural Computation* 4, no. 1 (1992): 1–58.

German Advisory Council for Consumer Affairs. *Consumer-Friendly Scoring*. 2019.

Gigerenzer, Gerd. "The Bias Bias in Behavioral Economics." *Review of Behavioral Economics*, no. 5 (2018): 303–336.

Gigerenzer, Gerd. *Calculated Risk: How to Know When Numbers Deceive You*. New York: Simon and Schuster, 2002.

Gigerenzer, Gerd. "From Tools to Theories: A Heuristic of Discovery in Cognitive Psychology." *Psychological Review* 98, no. 2 (1991): 254–267.

Gigerenzer, Gerd. *Gut Feelings: The Intelligence of the Unconscious*. New York: Penguin, 2007.

Gigerenzer, Gerd. "The Heuristics Revolution: Rethinking the Role of Uncertainty in Finance." In *The Behavioral Finance Revolution: A New Approach to Financial Policies and Regulations*, ed. Riccardo Viale, Shabnam Mousavi, Barbara Alemanni, and Umberto Filotto, 115–134. Cheltenham: Edward Elgar, 2018.

Gigerenzer, Gerd. "Ideas in Exile: The Struggles of an Upright Man." In *The Essential Brunswik: Beginnings, Explications, Applications*, ed. Kenneth R. Hammond and Tom R. Stewart, 445–452. Oxford: Oxford University Press, 2001.

Gigerenzer, Gerd. *Risk Savvy: How to Make Good Decisions*. New York: Viking, 2014.

Gigerenzer, Gerd. "What Is Bounded Rationality?" In *Routledge Handbook of Bounded Rationality*, ed. Riccardo Viale. London: Routledge, in press.

Gigerenzer, Gerd, and Henry Brighton. "Homo Heuristicus: Why Biased Minds Make Better Inferences." *Topics in Cognitive Science* 1, no. 1 (2009): 107–143.

Gigerenzer, Gerd, and Daniel G. Goldstein. "Reasoning the Fast and Frugal Way: Models of Bounded Rationality." *Psychological Review*, no. 103 (1996): 650–669.

Gigerenzer, Gerd, Ralph Hertwig, and Thorsten Pachur, eds. *Heuristics: The Foundations of Adaptive Behavior*. New York: Oxford University Press, 2011.

Gigerenzer, Gerd, and David J. Murray. *Cognition as Intuitive Statistics*. London: Psychology Press, 2015.

Gigerenzer, Gerd, and Reinhard Selten, eds. *Bounded Rationality: The Adaptive Toolbox*. Cambridge, MA: MIT Press, 2001.

Gigerenzer, Gerd, and Thomas Sturm. "How (Far) Can Rationality Be Naturalized?" *Synthese*, no. 187 (2012): 243–268.

Gigerenzer, Gerd, Peter M. Todd, and the ABC Research Group. *Simple Heuristics That Make Us Smart*. New York: Oxford University Press, 1999.

Ginsberg, Jeremy, Matthew H. Mohebbi, Rajan S. Patel, Lynnette Brammer, Mark S. Smolinski, and Larry Brilliant. "Detecting Influenza Epidemics Using Search Engine Query Data." *Nature* 457, no. 7232 (2009): 1012–1014.

Glymour, Clark. "Osiander's Psychology." *Behavioral and Brain Sciences* 34, no. 4 (2011): 200.

Goel, Sharad, Jake M. Hofman, Sébastien Lahaie, David M. Pennock, and Duncan J. Watts. "Predicting Consumer Behavior with Web Search." *Proceedings of the National Academy of Sciences* 107, no. 41 (2010): 17486–17490.

Green, Lee, and David R. Mehr. "What Alters Physicians' Decisions to Admit to the Coronary Care Unit?" *Journal of Family Practice* 45, no. 3 (1997): 219–226.

Gregg, Lee W., and Herbert A. Simon. "Process Models and Stochastic Theories of Simple Concept Formation." *Journal of Mathematical Psychology* 4, no. 2 (1967): 246–276.

Grimes, Derek I., John Rawcliffe, Jeannine Smith, LTC Eugene Baime, LTC Michael Benjamin, MAJ James Dorn, MAJ Chris Fredrikson, et al. *Operational Law Handbook*. Charlottesville, VA: International and Operational Law Department, Judge Advocate General's Legal Center and School, 2006.

Haldane, Andrew G., and Vasileios Madouros. "The Dog and the Frisbee." *Revista de Economia Institucional*, no. 14 (2012): 109–110.

Hamlin, Robert P. "The Gaze Heuristic: Biography of an Adaptively Rational Decision Process." *Topics in Cognitive Science* 9, no. 2 (2017): 264–288.

Hammond, D. "The Effects of Remand." *Prison Service Journal*, no. 69 (1988): 19.

Härle, Philipp, Erik Lüders, Theo Pepanides, Sonja Pfetsch, Thomas Poppensieker, and Uwe Stegemann. "Basel III and European Banking: Its Impact, How Banks Might Respond, and the Challenges of Implementation." McKinsey Working Papers on Risk no. 26 (November 2010).

Hertwig, Ralph, Jennifer Nerissa Davis, and Frank J. Sulloway. "Parental Investment: How an Equity Motive Can Produce Inequality." *Psychological Bulletin* 128, no. 5 (2002): 728–745.

Hertwig, Ralph, Ulrich Hoffrage, and the ABC Research Group. *Simple Heuristics in a Social World*. New York: Oxford University Press, 2013.

Hertwig, Ralph, Timothy J. Pleskac, Thorsten Pachur, and the Center for Adaptive Rationality. *Taming Uncertainty*. Cambridge, MA: MIT Press, 2019.

Hogarth, Robin M. "When Simple Is Hard to Accept." In *Ecological Rationality: Intelligence in the World*, by Peter M. Todd, Gerd Gigerenzer, and the ABC Research Group, 61–79. New York: Oxford University Press, 2012.

Holewinski, Sarah. "Escalation of Force: The Civilian Perspective." In *Escalation of Force Handbook*, 81–82. Fort Leavenworth, KS: Center for Army Lessons Learned, 2007.

Human Rights Watch. *China: Police "Big Data" Systems Violate Privacy, Target Dissent.* 2017.

Hunter, David A. "The Conservation and Demography of the Southern Corroboree Frog." MA thesis, University of Canberra, 2000.

Hutchinson, John M. C., and Gerd Gigerenzer. "Simple Heuristics and Rules of Thumb: Where Psychologists and Behavioural Biologists Might Meet." *Behavioural Processes* 69, no. 2 (2005): 97–124.

Jenny, Mirjam A., Niklas Keller, and Gerd Gigerenzer. "Assessing Minimal Medical Statistical Literacy Using the Quick Risk Test: A Prospective Observational Study in Germany." *British Medical Journal Open* 8, no. 8 (2018): e020847.

Jenny, Mirjam A., Thorsten Pachur, S. Lloyd Williams, Eni Becker, and Jürgen Margraf. "Simple Rules for Detecting Depression." *Journal of Applied Research in Memory and Cognition* 2, no. 3 (2013): 149–157.

Karaliopoulos, Merkourios, Konstantinos V. Katsikopoulos, and Lambros Lambrinos. "Bounded Rationality Can Make Parking Search More Efficient: The Power of Lexicographic Heuristics." *Transportation Research Part B: Methodological* 101 (2017): 28–50.

Karaliopoulos, Merkourios, and Iordanis Koutsopoulos. "Mobile App User Choice Engineering Using Behavioral Science Models." In *2018 IEEE 19th International*

Workshop on Signal Processing Advances in Wireless Communications (Piscataway: IEEE, 2018): 1–5.

Katsikopoulos, Konstantinos V. "How to Model It: Review of 'Cognitive Modeling.'" *Journal of Mathematical Psychology* 55, no. 2 (2011): 198–201.

Katsikopoulos, Konstantinos V. "Psychological Heuristics for Making Inferences: Definition, Performance, and the Emerging Theory and Practice." *Decision Analysis* 8, no. 1 (2011): 10–29.

Katsikopoulos, Konstantinos V., Ian N. Durbach, and Theodor J. Stewart. "When Should We Use Simple Decision Models? A Synthesis of Various Research Strands." *Omega* 81 (2018): 17–25.

Katsikopoulos, Konstantinos V., and Laura Martignon. "Naive Heuristics for Paired Comparisons: Some Results on Their Relative Accuracy." *Journal of Mathematical Psychology* 50, no. 3 (2006): 488–494.

Kay, John, and Mervyn King. *Radical Uncertainty: Decision-Making Beyond the Numbers*. New York: W. W. Norton, 2020.

Keller, Niklas, and Konstantinos V. Katsikopoulos. "On the Role of Psychological Heuristics in Operational Research; and a Demonstration in Military Stability Operations." *European Journal of Operational Research* 249, no. 3 (2016): 1063–1073.

Kirchner, Lauren. "Traces of Crime: How New York's DNA Techniques Became Tainted." *New York Times*, September 4, 2017.

Kirchner, Lauren. "Where Traditional DNA Testing Fails, Algorithms Take Over." *ProPublica*, November 4, 2016.

Klein, Gary A. *Sources of Power: How People Make Decisions*. Cambridge, MA: MIT Press, 1998.

Knight, Frank. *Risk, Uncertainty and Profit*. Boston, MA: Houghton Mifflin, 1921.

Kocher, Mininder S., Rahul Mandiga, David Zurakowski, Carol Barnewolt, and James R. Kasser. "Validation of a Clinical Prediction Rule for the Differentiation between Septic Arthritis and Transient Synovitis of the Hip in Children." *Journal of Bone and Joint Surgery* 86, no. 8 (2004): 1629–1635.

Kruschke, John K. "Models of Categorization." In *The Cambridge Handbook of Computational Psychology*, ed. Ron Sun. New York: Cambridge University Press, 2008.

Kumar, Neeraj, Alexander C. Berg, Peter N. Belhumeur, and Shree K. Nayar. "Attribute and Simile Classifiers for Face Verification." In *2009 IEEE 12th International Conference on Computer Vision* (Piscataway: IEEE, 2009), 365–372.

Lake, Brenden M., Tomer D. Ullman, Joshua B. Tenenbaum, and Samuel J. Gershman. "Building Machines That Learn and Think Like People." *Behavioral and Brain Sciences* 40 (2017): e253.

Larsen, Peter Thal. "Goldman Pays the Price of Being Big." *Financial Times*, March 13, 2007.

Larson, Christina. "China's AI Imperative: The Country's Massive Investments in Artificial Intelligence Are Disrupting the Industry—and Strengthening Control of the Populace." *Science* 359, no. 6376 (2018): 628–630.

Larson, Jeff, Surya Mattu, Lauren Kirchner, and Julia Angwin. "How We Analyzed the COMPAS Recidivism Algorithm." *ProPublica*, May 23, 2016, 5–9.

Lazer, David, Ryan Kennedy, Gary King, and Alessandro Vespignani. "The Parable of Google Flu: Traps in Big Data Analysis." *Science* 343, no. 6176 (2014): 1203–1205.

LeCun, Yann, Léon Bottou, Yoshua Bengio, and Patrick Haffner. "Gradient-Based Learning Applied to Document Recognition." *Proceedings of the IEEE* (1998).

Lessmann, Stefan, Bart Baesens, Hsin-Vonn Seow, and Lyn C. Thomas. "Benchmarking State-of-the-Art Classification Algorithms for Credit Scoring: An Update of Research." *European Journal of Operational Research* 247, no. 1 (2015): 124–136.

Letham, Benjamin, Cynthia Rudin, Tyler H. McCormick, and David Madigan. "Interpretable Classifiers Using Rules and Bayesian Analysis: Building a Better Stroke Prediction Model." *Annals of Applied Statistics* 9, no. 3 (2015): 1350–1371.

Liang Fan, Vishnupriya Das, Nadiya Kostyuk, and Muzammil M. Hussain. "Constructing a Data- Driven Society: China's Social Credit System as a State Surveillance Infrastructure." *Policy and Internet* 4 (2018).

Lichtman, Alan J. *Predicting the Next President: The Keys to the White House.* Lanham, MD: Rowman and Littlefield, 2016.

Lim, Wei S., Menno M. Van der Eerden, Richard T. R. Laing, Wim G. Boersma, Noel Karalus, George I. Town, et al. "Defining Community Acquired Pneumonia Severity on Presentation to Hospital: An International Derivation and Validation Study." *Thorax* 58, no. 5 (2003): 377–382.

Luan, Shenghua, and Jochen Reb. "Fast-and-Frugal Trees as Noncompensatory Models of Performance-Based Personnel Decisions." *Organizational Behavior and Human Decision Processes* 141 (2017): 29–42.

Luan, Shenghua, Lael J. Schooler, and Gerd Gigerenzer. "A Signal-Detection Analysis of Fast-and-Frugal Trees." *Psychological Review* 118, no. 2 (2011): 316–338.

Marcus, Gary, and Ernest Davis. "How to Build Artificial Intelligence We Can Trust." *New York Times International Edition*, September 11, 2019.

Martignon, Laura, Konstantinos V. Katsikopoulos, and Jan K. Woike. "Categorization with Limited Resources: A Family of Simple Heuristics." *Journal of Mathematical Psychology* 52, no. 6 (2008): 352–361.

Martignon, Laura, Oliver Vitouch, Masanori Takezawa, and Malcolm R. Forster. "Naive and Yet Enlightened: From Natural Frequencies to Fast and Frugal Decision Trees." In *Thinking: Psychological Perspectives on Reasoning, Judgment, and Decision Making*, ed. Laura Macchi and David Hardman, 189–211. Hoboken, NJ: John Wiley and Sons, 2003.

Medin, Douglas L., and Marguerite M. Schaffer. "Context Theory of Classification Learning." *Psychological Review* 85, no. 3 (1978): 207–238.

Montgomery, Nancy. "U.S. Seeks to Reduce Civilian Deaths at Iraq Checkpoints." *Stars and Stripes*, March 18, 2006.

Morgan, James N., and John A. Sonquist. "Problems in the Analysis of Survey Data, and a Proposal." *Journal of the American Statistical Association* 58, no. 302 (1963): 415–434.

Moyer, Virginia A. "Screening for HIV: US Preventive Services Task Force Recommendation Statement." *Annals of Internal Medicine* 159, no. 1 (2013): 51–60.

Musgrave, Alan. "Logical versus Historical Theories of Confirmation." *British Journal for the Philosophy of Science* 25, no. 1 (1974): 1–23.

Naik, Aanand D., Felicia Skelton, Amber B. Amspoker, Russell A. Glasgow, and Barbara W. Trautner. "A Fast and Frugal Algorithm to Strengthen Diagnosis and Treatment Decisions for Catheter-Associated Bacteriuria." *PLOS One* 12, no. 3 (2017): e0174415.

Nosofsky, Robert M., and Thomas J. Palmeri. "An Exemplar-Based Random Walk Model of Speeded Classification." *Psychological Review* 104, no. 2 (1997): 266–300.

Nosofsky, Robert M., Thomas J. Palmeri, and Stephen C. McKinley. "Rule-Plus-Exception Model of Classification Learning." *Psychological Review* 101, no. 1 (1994): 53–79.

Olson, Donald R., Kevin J. Konty, Marc Paladini, Cecile Viboud, and Lone Simonsen. "Reassessing Google Flu Trends Data for Detection of Seasonal and Pandemic Influenza: A Comparative Epidemiological Study at Three Geographic Scales." *PLOS Computational Biology* 9, no. 10 (2013): e1003256.

Payne, John W., James R. Bettman, and Eric J. Johnson. *The Adaptive Decision Maker*. Cambridge: Cambridge University Press, 1993.

Phillips, Nathaniel D., Hansjörg Neth, Jan K. Woike, and Wolfgang Gaissmaier. "FFTrees: A Toolbox to Create, Visualize, and Evaluate Fast-and-Frugal Decision Trees." *Judgment and Decision Making* 12, no. 4 (2017): 344–368.

Pisters, Ron, Deirdre A. Lane, Robby Nieuwlaat, Cees B. De Vos, Harry J. G. M. Crijns, and Gregory YH Lip. "A Novel User-Friendly Score (HAS-BLED) to Assess 1-Year Risk of Major Bleeding in Patients with Atrial Fibrillation: The Euro Heart Survey." *Chest* 138, no. 5 (2010): 1093–1100.

Pitt, Mark A., and In Jae Myung. "When a Good Fit Can Be Bad." *Trends in Cognitive Sciences* 6, no. 10 (2002): 421–425.

Pollan, Michael. *Food Rules: An Eater's Manual.* New York: Penguin, 2009.

Pozen, Michael W., Ralph B. D'Agostino, Harry P. Selker, Pamela A. Sytkowski, and William B. Hood Jr. "A Predictive Instrument to Improve Coronary-Care-Unit Admission Practices in Acute Ischemic Heart Disease: A Prospective Multicenter Clinical Trial." *New England Journal of Medicine* 310, no. 20 (1984): 1273–1278.

Prasad, Vinay, Jeanne Lenzer, and David H. Newman. "Why Cancer Screening Has Never Been Shown to 'Save Lives'—and What We Can Do about It." *British Medical Journal* 352 (2016): h6080.

Prinz, Roman, Markus Feufel, Gerd Gigerenzer, and Odette Wegwarth. "What Counselors Tell Low-Risk Clients about HIV Test Performance." *Current HIV Research* 13, no. 5 (2015): 369–380.

Quinlan, J. Ross. *C4.5: Programs for Machine Learning.* Amsterdam, Netherlands: Elsevier, 1993.

Quinn, Paul C. "Beyond Prototypes." In *Advances in Child Development and Behavior*, ed. R. V. Kai and H. W. Reese, 161–193. San Diego: Academic Press, 2002.

Quinn, Paul C., Peter D. Eimas, and Michael J. Tarr. "Perceptual Categorization of Cat and Dog Silhouettes by 3- to 4-Month-Old Infants." *Journal of Experimental Child Psychology* 79, no. 1 (2001): 78–94.

Rakison, David H., and Lisa M. Oakes, eds. *Early Category and Concept Development: Making Sense of the Blooming, Buzzing Confusion.* Oxford: Oxford University Press, 2003.

Rivest, Ronald L. "Learning Decision Lists." *Machine Learning* 2, no. 3 (1987): 229–246.

Roberts, Seth, and Harold Pashler. "How Persuasive Is a Good Fit? A Comment on Theory Testing." *Psychological Review* 107, no. 2 (2000): 358–367.

Romig, Lou E. "Pediatric Triage: A System to JumpSTART Your Triage of Young Patients at MCIs." *Journal of Emergency Medical Services* 27, no. 7 (2002): 52–58.

Rubinstein, Reuven. "The Cross-Entropy Method for Combinatorial and Continuous Optimization." *Methodology and Computing in Applied Probability* 1, no. 2 (1999): 127–190.

Rudin, Cynthia, and Joanna Radin. "Why Are We Using Black Box Models in AI When We Don't Need To? A Lesson from an Explainable AI Competition." *Harvard Data Science Review* 1, no. 2 (2019).

Sanborn, Adam N., and Nick Chater. "Bayesian Brains without Probabilities." *Trends in Cognitive Sciences* 20, no. 12 (2016): 883–893.

Savage, Leonard J. *The Foundations of Statistics*. Mineola, NY: Dover, 1954.

Schroff, Florian, Dmitry Kalenichenko, and James Philbin. "Facenet: A Unified Embedding for Face Recognition and Clustering." In *Proceedings of the IEEE Conference on Computer Vision and Pattern Recognition*, 815–823 (Piscataway: IEEE, 2015).

Seymour, Christopher W., Vincent X. Liu, Theodore J. Iwashyna, Frank M. Brunkhorst, Thomas D. Rea, André Scherag, Gordon Rubenfeld et al. "Assessment of Clinical Criteria for Sepsis for the Third International Consensus Definitions for Sepsis and Septic Shock (Sepsis-3)." *Journal of the American Medical Association* 315, no. 8 (2016): 762–774.

Silver, David, Thomas Hubert, Julian Schrittwieser, Ioannis Antonoglou, Matthew Lai, Arthur Guez, Marc Lanctot et al. "A General Reinforcement Learning Algorithm That Masters Chess, Shogi, and Go through Self-Play." *Science* 362, no. 6419 (2018): 1140–1144.

Silver, David, et al. "Mastering the Game of Go without Human Knowledge." *Nature* 550, no. 7676 (2017): 354–359.

Simon, Herbert A. *Models of Bounded Rationality: Empirically Grounded Economic Reason*. Cambridge, MA: MIT Press, 1997.

Simon, Herbert A. "Rational Choice and the Structure of the Environment." *Psychological Review* 63, no. 2 (1956): 129–138.

Simonoff, Jeffrey S. *Analyzing Categorical Data*. New York: Springer, 2003.

Şimşek, Özgür. "Linear Decision Rule as Aspiration for Simple Decision Heuristics." *Advances in Neural Information Processing Systems* (2013): 2904–2912.

Şimşek, Özgür, and Marcus Buckmann. "Learning from Small Samples: An Analysis of Simple Decision Heuristics." In *Advances in Neural Information Processing Systems* 28 (2015): 3159–3167.

Sinha, Pawan, Benjamin J. Balas, Yuri Ostrovsky, and Richard Russell. *Face Recognition: Models and Mechanism*. Cambridge, MA: Academic Press, 2003.

Smith, Jack W., J. E. Everhart, W. C. Dickson, W. C. Knowler, and R. S. Johannes. "Using the ADAP Learning Algorithm to Forecast the Onset of Diabetes Mellitus." In *Proceedings of the Annual Symposium on Computer Application in Medical Care* (American Medical Informatics Association, 1988), 261.

Smith, Liz, and Ken Gilhooly. "Regression versus Fast and Frugal Models of Decision-Making: The Case of Prescribing for Depression." *Applied Cognitive Psychology: The Official Journal of the Society for Applied Research in Memory and Cognition* 20, no. 2 (2006): 265–274.

State Council. "Planning Outline for the Construction of a Social Credit System (2014–2020)." *China Copyright and Media*, June 14, 2014.

Sterelny, Kim. *Thought in a Hostile World: The Evolution of Human Cognition*. Hoboken, NJ: Wiley Blackwell, 2003.

Stiglitz, Joseph E. *Freefall: America, Free Markets, and the Sinking of the World Economy*. New York: W. W. Norton, 2010.

Super, Gary. *START: A Triage Training Module*. Newport Beach, CA: Hoag Memorial Hospital Presbyterian, 1984.

Taleb, Nassim Nicholas. *Skin in the Game: Hidden Asymmetries in Daily Life*. New York: Allen Lane, 2018.

Tan, Jolene H., Shenghua Luan, and Konstantinos V. Katsikopoulos. "A Signal-Detection Approach to Modeling Forgiveness Decisions." *Evolution and Human Behavior* 38, no. 1 (2017): 27–38.

Tanner, Wilson P., Jr., and John A. Swets. "A Decision-Making Theory of Visual Detection." *Psychological Review* 61, no. 6 (1954): 401–409.

Thompson, William C., Franco Taroni, and Colin G. G. Aitken. "How the Probability of a False Positive Affects the Value of DNA Evidence." *Journal of Forensic Science* 48, no. 1 (2003): 1–8.

Todd, Peter M., Gerd Gigerenzer, and the ABC Research Group. *Ecological Rationality: Intelligence in the World*. New York: Oxford University Press, 2012.

Trafimow, David. "Hypothesis Testing and Theory Evaluation at the Boundaries: Surprising Insights from Bayes's Theorem." *Psychological Review* 110, no. 3 (2003): 526–535.

Tukey, John Wilder. *Exploratory Data Analysis*. Boston, MA: Addison-Wesley, 1970.

Tversky, Amos. "Elimination by Aspects: A Theory of Choice." *Psychological Review* 79, no. 4 (1972): 281–299.

Tversky, Amos, and Daniel Kahneman. "Judgment under Uncertainty: Heuristics and Biases." *Science* 185, no. 4157 (1974): 1124–1131.

United Nations Assistance Mission to Afghanistan. *Human Rights' Group Annual Report on the Protection of Civilians in Armed Conflict*. Kabul, Afghanistan, 2012.

US Preventive Services Task Force. "Screening for Skin Cancer: US Preventive Services Task Force Recommendation Statement." *Annals of Internal Medicine* 150, no. 3 (2009): 429.

van Rooij, Tibor, Mary Roederer, Todd Wareham, Iris van Rooij, Howard L. McLeod, and Sharon Marsh. "Fast and Frugal Trees: Translating Population-Based Pharmacogenomics to Medication Prioritization." *Personalized Medicine* 12, no. 2 (2015): 117–128.

Wald, Abraham. *Statistical Decision Functions*. New York: Wiley, 1950.

Welch, Gilbert H., Steven Woloshin, and Lisa M. Schwartz. "Skin Biopsy Rates and Incidence of Melanoma: Population-Based Ecological Study." *British Medical Journal* 331, no. 7515 (2005): 481.

Woike, Jan K., Ulrich Hoffrage, and Jeffrey S. Petty. "Picking Profitable Investments: The Success of Equal Weighting in Simulated Venture Capitalist Decision Making." *Journal of Business Research* 68, no. 8 (2015): 1705–1716.

Wübben, Markus, and Florian V. Wangenheim. "Instant Customer Base Analysis: Managerial Heuristics Often 'Get It Right.'" *Journal of Marketing* 72, no. 3 (2008): 82–93.

Zhao, Sihai Dave, Giovanni Parmigiani, Curtis Huttenhower, and Levi Waldron. "Más-o-Menos: A Simple Sign Averaging Method for Discrimination in Genomic Data Analysis." *Bioinformatics* 30, no. 21 (2014): 3062–3069.

Zięba, Maciej, Sebastian K. Tomczak, and Jakub M. Tomczak. "Ensemble Boosted Trees with Synthetic Features Generation in Application to Bankruptcy Prediction." *Expert Systems with Applications* 58 (2016): 93–101.

Author Index

Subject Index